The Dangerous AI Gamble in Education

By Dr Finn Majlergaard

Published by

GUGINPRESS, 127 Rue Cagnoli, 06450 Saint Martin Vesubie, FRANCE.

https://guginpress.fr

ISBN 978-2-9564665-0-5 (Paper)
ISBN 978-2-9564665-1-2 (eBook)

First edition 2025

Printed by:

Preface

When tech companies take over education, profit comes first - and students lose everything.

The tech industry has set its sights on education—and the stakes could not be higher. Behind promises of efficiency and innovation lies a strategy to reshape schools and universities on their terms, not ours. These companies care only about profit, no matter what they destroy along the way - even the values and traditions that make education a cornerstone of society.

This book exposes why AI can be dangerous in the classroom when left in the hands of corporations, and why it is essential for educators to set clear policies and boundaries before adopting any new technology.

I wrote this book for professors, teachers, and educational institutions to show you how to cut through the sales tactics and seductive pitches of tech giants, and how to defend what truly matters: your students, your teaching, and the integrity of education itself. I do not want to see great education—built over centuries of dedication, wisdom, and human connection—destroyed by an overhyped technology that promises shortcuts but risks eroding the very values that make learning meaningful.

I want to avoid a future where Big Tech dismantles the education sector in pursuit of profit. That is why we must remain critical of artificial intelligence and resist the temptation to accept glossy sales pitches that are often unsupported and undocumented. It is frighteningly easy to undermine what generations have created, and once lost, the depth, richness, and humanity of education cannot easily be rebuilt.

With the knowledge I have gained over many years of research and practical experience in cultural and emotional intelligence, I know just how fragile a good culture and a healthy learning environment can be—and how quickly they can be destroyed. That is why we must remain vigilant and critical of artificial intelligence, which today is driven far more by commercial interests and Big Tech's agenda than by genuine educational needs. Protecting education means resisting these pressures and putting human values before technological hype.

It is essential that we regard AI only as a tool—and nothing more. Yet tech companies are aggressively trying to position themselves at the very center of education, reducing professors and teachers to nothing more than "learning coaches." We must never allow this shift to happen. If we do, we risk repeating the same disasters we have already witnessed with social media: rising stress, growing loneliness, and declining learning outcomes. The warning signs are already here, and in this book I draw on these experiences to show why we must act before it is too late.

m available as a thought-provoking keynote speaker, an engaging workshop facilitator, an AI strategy coach, and for media interviews.

I will be looking forward hearing from yourself

Dr Finn MAJLERGAARD

Table of contents

Table of Contents

Introduction

The 12-Watt Wonder vs. The Billion-Watt Beast

Right now, as you read these words, your brain is humming along on the same power it takes to run a dim light bulb—just 12 watts. Meanwhile, the AI systems everyone's buzzing about? They're gulping down 2.7 billion watts to process that same sentence. That's like comparing a hummingbird to a cargo plane trying to hover at your window.

So here's the million-euro question: If We are already running circles around AI with the energy efficiency of a digital watch, why are we convinced these power-hungry machines are about to revolutionise everything?

The answer isn't in the technology—it's in the sales pitch.

You have nothing to fear from artificial intelligence itself. The real threat? The politicians promising AI utopias and the tech salespeople who've convinced us that bigger, hungrier, and more expensive automatically means better.

Welcome to the reality check our silicon-obsessed world desperately needs.

A wake-up call for educators, administrators, and anyone who cares about the future of learning

"Your students are being watched, measured, and sorted by algorithms you don't understand, using data you can't see, for purposes you haven't approved. And the companies selling these systems want you to believe this is progress."

The Seductive Promise and the Hidden Price

Artificial intelligence has arrived in education with grand promises: personalised learning paths, instant feedback, automated grading, and the liberation of teachers from mundane tasks. Tech companies paint a picture of educational utopia where every student receives perfectly tailored instruction, where learning is optimised, and where human potential is maximised through the power of algorithms.

But what if this promise is not just overhyped—what if it's fundamentally dangerous?

This book cuts through the marketing rhetoric to reveal what AI in education actually does, how it really works, and why the cure might be worse than the disease. After 25 years as a professor witnessing the transformation of students from curious learners into algorithm-dependent consumers of content, I have seen enough to sound the alarm.

The Students Who Can't Think for Themselves

Picture this: A student delivers a flawless presentation on quantum physics, complete with sophisticated arguments and cutting-edge research. The audience is impressed. The professor is pleased. There's just one problem—the student can barely read the words on their own slides, let alone understand the concepts they're supposedly explaining.

This isn't a hypothetical scenario. It's happening in classrooms around the world, right now. Personally I have experienced it a number of times and when I confront the students with my strong suspicion that their presentation is merely output from a LLM they sometimes don't even see, that it is wrong. That makes me think seriously about what kind of people we are making? But of course, one way to make AI systems look smart is by making the humans dumper. AI tools are creating a generation of students who mistake access to information for understanding, who confuse speed for intelligence, and who are losing the very capacity to think critically that education is supposed to develop.

A Recent [MIT Brain chatGPT Study] reveals something shocking: intensive use of AI tools like ChatGPT is literally changing how students' brains function. The implications are staggering, yet We are rushing headlong into AI adoption without stopping to ask what We are sacrificing in the process.

Here is what they found out

The researchers at MIT examined how the brain functions when people write essays with and without artificial intelligence.

They compared three groups: those using ChatGPT, those using Google, and those relying solely on their own knowledge without using any technology. Across four essay-writing sessions, brain activity was measured with EEG. The unaided group showed the strongest and most widely distributed neural connectivity, the Google group engaged moderately, and the ChatGPT users demonstrated the weakest activity, particularly in the alpha and beta wave bands linked to working memory and problem-solving. Reliance on ChatGPT therefore reduced cognitive effort during the task. When participants switched conditions, those moving from ChatGPT to unaided writing still showed suppressed brain activity, suggesting a lingering effect.

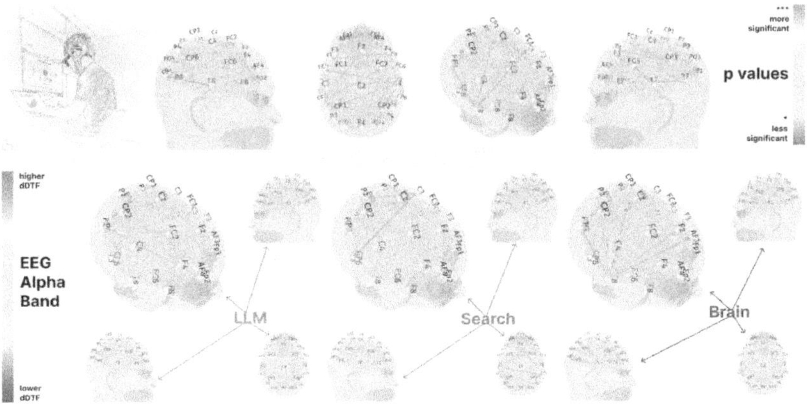

Figure 2: EEG connectivity differences across essay-writing methods. Reprinted from Kosmyna, N., Maes, P., Ochoa, X., Han, C., & Caggianese, G. (2025). Your brain on ChatGPT: Accumulation of cognitive debt when using an AI assistant for essay writing task. arXiv. https://doi.org/10.48550/arXiv.2506.08872

Figure 1: Brain activity using LLM; Google or just brain

Conversely, those moving from unaided writing to ChatGPT quickly reduced their mental effort. Essay analysis revealed that ChatGPT texts were polished but lacked originality and personal voice, and many users could not recall or quote their own work. That is also one of the reason why I have chosen this subtitle for this book: "*When AI teaches, students have nothing meaningful to say*". The researched people also felt less ownership of what they had written, unlike those in the unaided group who retained stronger memory of their output. The researchers described this as "cognitive debt": the mental cost of outsourcing thinking to AI. Just as financial debt accumulates with borrowing, repeated reliance on AI may erode memory, learning, and creativity. The authors warn that overuse of AI in education risks undermining critical skills and urge caution before embedding such tools deeply in teaching and assessment.

I always provoke my students and I have no problem taking on points of views, that are not mine, just for the sake of provocation. I have always done it because critical thinking is one of the most important skills we can develop in our students. My fear is that AI can turn students into passive learners who absorbs anything presented to them – hence this critical book!

The Surveillance State Comes to School

Every click, every pause, every answer—AI systems in education are collecting unprecedented amounts of data about our students. They're building detailed psychological profiles, tracking behavioural patterns, and making predictions about future performance. But here's what they are not doing: telling you exactly what data they are collecting, how they are using it, or who they are sharing it with. I find that deeply concerning.

Educational AI systems operate as black boxes, offering neither transparency nor accountability. They promise individualised learning but deliver an algorithmic conformity just like when you are searching for an accommodation on a booking portal. They never come up with crazy new suggestion to push you outside your traditional patterns. Netflix doesn't suggest you to see a different kind of films because you have seen a lot of the same kind of films, and it will not propose you to switch off the TV and read a book instead.

Your spouse or friend would do that, but never an AI system. The AI systems in education claim to support teachers but systematically replace human judgment with automated decision-making. These AI systems are marketed as innovative solutions while continue to create the same old problems - and creating dangerous new ones as well

The Recommendation Engine Trap

I think that one of the most sneaky features of educational AI isn't its mistakes - it's when it works exactly as designed. These systems use recommendation algorithms similar to those that keep you scrolling on social media, but instead of trapping you with cat videos, they're trapping students in narrow learning pathways. As a professor you can always recommend students some thought-provoking reading which may only associate remotely to the topic of the course, but it might have a more diffuse purpose only you as a professor know. It could for instance be suggesting an ego-centric student to learn basic emotional intelligence.

If for instance a student is skilled in mathematics, the AI doubles down, providing more and more mathematical content while steering them away from literature, arts, or interdisciplinary thinking. These systems don't broaden horizons - they narrow them. They don't encourage exploration - they reinforce existing patterns.

The result? Students who become increasingly specialised and decreasingly creative, innovative, and adaptable. Add to that what happens with the brain activity when using LLM intensively.

Is it that kind of students we want?

The Loneliness Epidemic Comes to Education

We've seen what happened when social media promised to connect us: despite being more "connected" than ever, We are experiencing unprecedented levels of loneliness, depression, and social isolation, particularly among young people. Educational AI is poised to repeat this catastrophic pattern.

A [Gallup-Meta Global Survey]found that 25% of the 15 to 18 year old felt that they were lonely and 27% of those between 19 and 29 years old said that they were very lonely or fairly lonely. That is a lot, and it is something that we need to take seriously. If we are using technologies in education the same way that we have used them in so-called social media, we will end up with tragic circumstances for the younger generation, not only because of social media, but also because they are becoming increasingly isolated using artificial intelligence when they are being educated. Somehow it is worse in Australia than anywhere else. 62% feel left out often or some of the time, and 58% feel isolated often or some of the time.

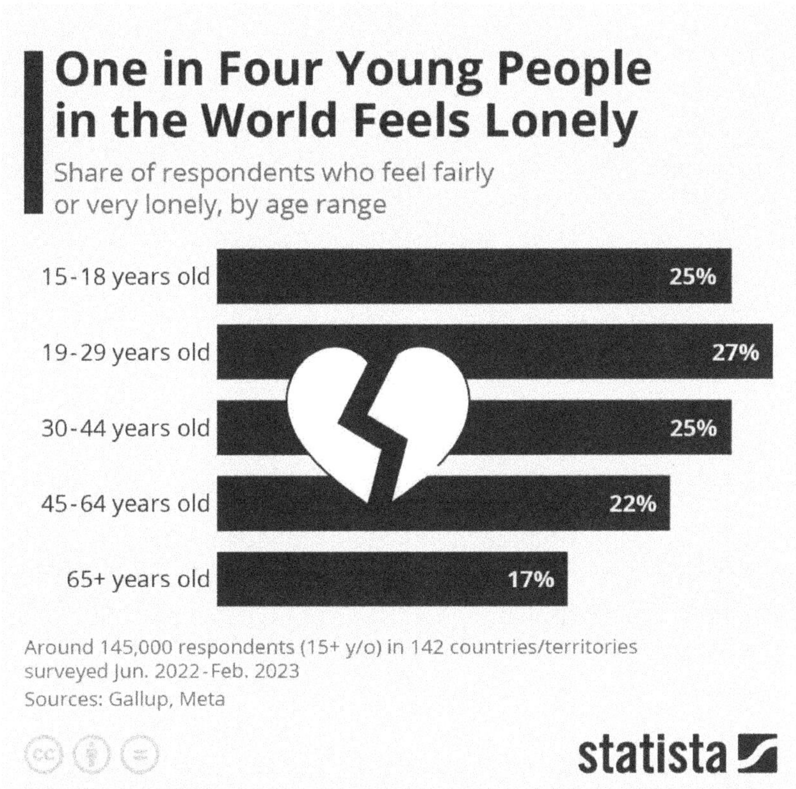

Figure 3: Statista GmbH. (2025). One in four young people in the world feels lonely [Chart]. Statista. Retrieved August 30, 2025, from Statista website.

If you are thinking back at your own childhood and youth - did you feel that way too?

We all have a responsibility, that this is not going to happen or get worse despite big-tech's pressure to promote their technologies and hi-jack all human-to-human connection.

By inserting algorithms between teachers/professors and students, AI systems are disrupting the fundamental human relationships that make learning meaningful. Students interact with chatbots instead of classmates, receive feedback from algorithms instead of mentors, and navigate learning paths designed by machines rather than educators who know and care about them as human beings.

The promise of "personalised learning" sounds appealing until you realise it often means "isolated learning" - each student alone with their screen, following their algorithmically determined personalised learning path, missing out on the collaborative, unplanned, dangerous, rule-breaking discovery, peer learning, and human connection that are essential to genuine education. I usually tell my business school students that the most important things they will learn are from all the unplanned, random events that force them to change direction or perceptions.

The Stress of Constant Surveillance

Imagine being monitored, measured, and evaluated every moment of every day. Every question you ask is recorded. Every wrong answer is analysed. Every pause in your work is interpreted as a sign of confusion, disengagement, or lack of ability. Life as a robot is really boring and frustrating.

This is the reality for students in AI-powered educational systems.

Research indicates that constant digital monitoring - through its unpredictability and intrusiveness - can induce technostress, manifested by chronic fatigue, burnout, and reduced motivation (Journal of Innovation & Knowledge, 2023). In young people, prolonged, unbuffered stress of any kind contributes to "toxic stress," where the stress response system becomes chronically activated, impairing emotional and cognitive development (Hormone Research in Paediatrics, 2023).

Yet We are implementing systems that turn every learning moment into a data point, every student into a subject of algorithmic analysis.

Why I'm Writing This Book

For the past quarter-century, I have been on the front lines of education as a professor of leadership, innovation, and change management at business schools around the world. I have supervised hundreds of PhD, MBA, and DBA students, many of whom are researching AI's impact on various fields. I have sat on committees selecting educational technologies and helped develop policies for AI implementation.

I have also spent years working in the big-tech industry, so I understand the sales tactics, the inflated promises, and the carefully obscured limitations that characterise how tech companies sell to educational institutions. I have seen how they target the least technically sophisticated decision-makers, how they influence policy at the highest levels, and how they create dependency before revealing the true costs.

Most importantly, I have witnessed the tragic human cost too often. I have watched intelligent students become dependent on AI tools they don't understand. I have seen creative thinkers reduced to prompt engineers. I have observed the gradual erosion of critical thinking skills, intellectual curiosity, and the kind of deep, sustained engagement that real learning requires.

We need to stop this maniac before it is too late. Once our young people have been damaged the recovery will be extremely difficult if possible at all.

A Different Path Forward

This book isn't a blanket condemnation of all technology in education. Not at all! It's a call for wisdom, caution, and putting human values before technological capabilities. There are ways to use AI responsibly in educational settings - but only if we understand what We are dealing with, insist on transparency, and refuse to let convenience and search for short-term profit override our core educational mission.

In the coming chapters you will learn how to evaluate AI tools critically, what questions to ask vendors, how to protect student privacy, and most importantly, how to preserve the essentially human elements of education that no algorithm can ever replicate.

The Choice Is Ours

The tech companies want us to believe that AI adoption in education is inevitable, that resistance is futile, and that we must adapt or be left behind. This is false! We do have choices. We can demand transparency. We can insist on human oversight. We can protect our students from algorithmic manipulation. We can preserve the irreplaceable value of human wisdom, creativity, and connection in learning.

But only if we act now, before the systems become so entrenched that changing course becomes impossible.

The future of education—and the minds of our students—hangs in the balance. This book will help you tip the scales toward human flourishing rather than technological control.

The choice is yours. The time is now.

Ready to challenge the AI revolution in education? Turn the page and discover what they don't want you to know...

1. The Great AI Deception in Education: What Revolution?

Artificial intelligence is being sold to us as the future of education. We are told it will make learning more efficient, more personal, and easier for teachers. But i am writing this book to tell you that this shiny promise hides some very serious problems that we need to talk about.

This book won't just accept that AI is good for education. Instead, I want us to look closely at the real risks - many of them quite serious - that come when we bring AI into classrooms and universities without thinking carefully about what We are doing.

Everyone talks about opportunities, but perhaps the truth is that AI threatens to damage some of the most important parts of education. When students use AI to write their essays, solve their homework, or answer exam questions, we have to ask: are they actually learning anything? When teachers use computer systems to mark work, sort students, or manage classes, are they really teaching?

What Education Really Means

Education isn't like a factory production line. It is not about getting the "right" answer or scoring well on a test. Real education is about learning to think for yourself and critically assess what is presented to you, to question things and evaluate alternatives, and to deal with complex ideas together with other people. AI - no matter how clever it seems - cannot do this. When we hand over the important parts of teaching and learning to machines, we risk creating students who might be good with technology but have nothing interesting to say, because we have a bad habit of becoming good at what we are measured by.

I am already seeing this happen. As a professor who studies how and why organisations change and how different cultures work together, and as someone who supervises doctoral students from around the world, I notice a worrying pattern. Nearly every of my PhD students today wants to research AI mixed with something else: AI and innovation, AI and business strategy, AI and ethics. But hardly any of them ask whether AI should be involved in these areas at all. And they don't question if AI really is as revolutionary as the tech companies claim. They seem to think AI is inevitable - so we just have to adapt. That is a really dangerous approach. They forget, we always have a choice! I try to remind them and provoke them.

Therefore, I don't accept that AI is a core component of almost everything we do. Fortunately I have been brought up to question everything, and that is what i intend to do with this book. Just because technology exists doesn't mean we have to use it. We have choices about how - or whether - we bring AI into our schools and universities. And we must not confuse what's convenient with what's actually progress. As I love to cook, I have a lot of very sharp knives in my kitchen. They can kill people but I don't use them for that so just because we have a tool or technology it doesn't mean we should use it for its most extreme use. AI is no different. We shall use it is a tool, nothing more.

The Trust Problem

One of the most obvious problems with AI in education is how it is destroying trust between students and teachers. Teachers increasingly suspect that students are handing in work written - or partly written by AI. Students, meanwhile, think their work is being unfairly judged or dismissed. The spirit of working together and learning together that should define higher education is being replaced by suspicion and spying on each other. This isn't a healthy way for people to learn and grow intellectually.

But it is not just about cheating. It is more worrying that AI is quietly changing what students think learning actually is. If the goal is simply to produce an essay that's grammatically correct, well-structured, and factually accurate, then yes, AI can help with that. But if the goal is to struggle with ideas, build arguments, question assumptions, make remote associations, express fears, hope and other feelings and develop good judgement that involves both cultural- and emotional intelligence - then getting machines to do our thinking for us is a massive step backwards.

I often ask my students if they are happy, and how they define happiness for themselves. They responses vary a lot depending on where I am in the world.

I have previously co-authored a book about how cultures are developing in emerging markets as they become more and more wealthy. And we can see that when economies are becoming more developed, the populations are also becoming more individualistic. So people, when they are not so rich, are thinking a more about their community, their family, their friends and their happiness as a group. Whereas when the economies become more developed, we see a rapid rise in individualism and a focus on getting financial wealth and not so much attention to being happy or feeling happy.

What does that have to do with artificial intelligence?

Well, I fear that the frontier markets in predominantly sub-Saharan Africa will adopt AI technologies quicker and more uncritically because the desire to show individual wealth and progress is so much more dominant than it is en more developed economies.

Furthermore, many educational institutions in that region, don't have the same financial strength as universities and business schools have in more developed economies. They they therefore be much easier to influence by the big-tech companies.

I fear, that this massive pressure will have catastrophic consequences for the students, their local communities and the countries. Later I will come back to some research that has been made on students who have been exposed AI learning tools over a longer period of time and the negative social, mental and intellectual consequences it has had.

The Job Crisis Nobody Talked About Before

The negative social, mental and cultural effects aren't limited to the classrooms. We are already seeing how AI is changing graduate employment. In fields like finance, law, and business consulting, entry-level analytical jobs are disappearing. AI systems can now do many of the tasks that used to be done by new graduates - faster, cheaper, and without complaining. This is creating a crisis, especially in countries where students graduate with huge debts and few chances of meaningful work.

In this context, the idea that AI will "free" us from boring tasks sounds hollow. For many young people, it is not freedom - it is being shut out completely. How are you ever going to become a valuable asset to a company or a country if you are shot out from the very beginning with a huge student debt? Who takes the responsibility for that?

Some teachers and professors are being encouraged to change their roles - from subject experts to facilitators or "learning coaches". This language is often used to justify replacing traditional teaching with AI-driven platforms. But teaching isn't a service that can be easily broken down into parts. It is a relationship, a conversation, a shared journey of discovery. Software cannot replicate that. The relationship between the professors and the students is based on trust. Developing that trust is a human connection and you can only lead the students through a development process if they trust you as a professor. The tech industry will like to hijack the connection between the professors and the students just like "social media" has hijacked the connection between people with the result that more people than ever before feel lonely and isolated. If we let a similar development happen in education students will become more stupid, more immature, more naive.

By suggesting that teachers and professors should become "learning coaches" the tech industry is sidelining the educators and make them naive spectators to the hostile tech-takeover.

The Manipulation Machine

And what about the systems behind these AI tools that promise to revolutionise our lives? The recommendation systems on platforms like Netflix, Amazon, YouTube, various booking portals and even educational apps are built to maximise engagement and profit - not to promote understanding or wisdom. They work by creating profiles of users and feeding them content that confirms what they already think and have a preference for. In doing so, they reinforce prejudices, narrow intellectual horizons, and discourage the kind of open-minded thinking that education should encourage.

Let me be clear: I am not afraid of technology. I have spent decades studying how organisations transform and advising companies around the world on managing organisational and cultural change. Many of these changes had to happen because of technological inventions that changed the competitive landscape. I am also the founder and CEO of Gugin, a global consultancy and leadership training firm focused on helping organisations create cultures where human intelligence isn't crushed by algorithmic control. But I am convinced that the enthusiastic embrace of AI in education - often in the name of efficiency or innovation - is dangerously premature. Most of the people promoting these systems have no clue what they are talking about. They are just sales representatives. You on the other hand, have the responsibility for the next generation.

These recommendation systems are also intransparent. We know from e.g. booking portals that the recommendations given to you are the ones where there is most profit to be made. They never come up with suggestions that will challenge your behavioural patterns and previous choices. If you are used to book 3-star hotels in the city centre it will never recommend you something new and thought-provoking e.g. a refurbished ship in the harbour or a lighthouse. You life will remain predictable and boring.

Tools Are Never Neutral

We must be wary of those who claim that AI is simply a tool. Tools are never neutral. They reshape the environments where they're used. As mentioned before, a knife can be used to for instance prepare food - or to harm someone. AI, likewise, reflects the values of those who design and use it. And since the core of an AI system is an intransparent black box, what guarantee do you have that it intentionally tries to indoctrinate you in one or the other way. We already know that for instance China is using AI intensively to influence people's behaviour and opinions through massive surveillance and tracking.

As we work through this book, we will explore not just what AI can do in education, but what it should do - if anything. I will examine how AI has developed, from its origins in wartime codebreaking and expert systems to today's large language models. I will question the assumptions that underpin its use. And I will challenge the myth that technology always equals progress.

The question isn't whether AI can improve learning outcomes or make things more efficient. The question is whether we are prepared to sacrifice the soul of education - critical thought, human connection, ethical reflection - in exchange for speed, profit and convenience. Are you ready to make that sacrifice?

There is still time to steer this movement in a better direction. But only if we stop treating AI as an inevitable destiny, and start treating it as a choice we can make. Don't forget – AI is predominantly a hype, fuelled by massive marketing.

Therefore, we need to keep the big-tech industry out of our analytical and decision processes. That starts with that we - each educational institution - must form its independent AI policies long before looking at potential technology is even considered. These policies must contain important promises to all the stakeholders, and all decisions you make have to stay within the frames of these policies.

2. Seeing Through the AI Hype -The Marketing Versus Reality

Have you ever thought about where AI actually comes from and when? You might be surprised to learn that artificial intelligence isn't as new as it is often made out to be. However, recent technological advances have of course given AI a considerable boost. Still, we must not confuse hype with progress, and we certainly shouldn't accept AI's expansion into education or society without serious questions we need to have answered particular around ethics, data-protection, transparency and accountability.

Artificial intelligence is much older than you may think

1940s	In 1943, neurophysiologist Warren McCulloch and mathematician Walter Pitts modeled how neurons might work using electrical circuits in a simple neural network.
1950s	The Turing test, proposed by Alan Turing in 1950, evaluates a machine's ability to exhibit intelligent behavior by having a human judge engage in text-based conversations with both a human and a machine without knowing which is which.
1960s	ELIZA, created by MIT's Joseph Weizenbaum in the mid-1960s, was the world's first chatbot that simulated conversation by using pattern matching and substitution to mimic a Rogerian psychotherapist.
1980s	In the 1980s, expert systems like MYCIN and DENDRAL emerged as early AI programs that used rule-based knowledge to mimic human expertise in specific domains such as medical diagnosis and chemical analysis.
1990s	In the 1990s, computer vision advanced significantly with the development of algorithms for object recognition, face detection, and image processing, enabled by increased computational power and digital imaging technology.
2000s	In the early 2000s, Google revolutionized web search with its PageRank algorithm that ranked pages by relevance and authority, while other search engines like Yahoo and AltaVista competed to organize the rapidly expanding internet.
2010s	In the 2010s, AI achieved major gaming milestones with IBM's Watson winning Jeopardy! in 2011, DeepMind's AlphaGo defeating world champion Lee Sedol at Go in 2016, and chess engines reaching superhuman levels of play.
2020s	In the 2020s, large language models like GPT-3 and GPT-4 demonstrated conversational abilities so sophisticated that some argued they could pass the Turing test, though debate continues over whether they truly exhibit human-level intelligence or sophisticated pattern matching.

List made by Dr Finn Majlergaard

Understanding What We Are Actually Dealing With

First, let's clarify the difference between artificial intelligence, automation, and human intelligence - because mix-

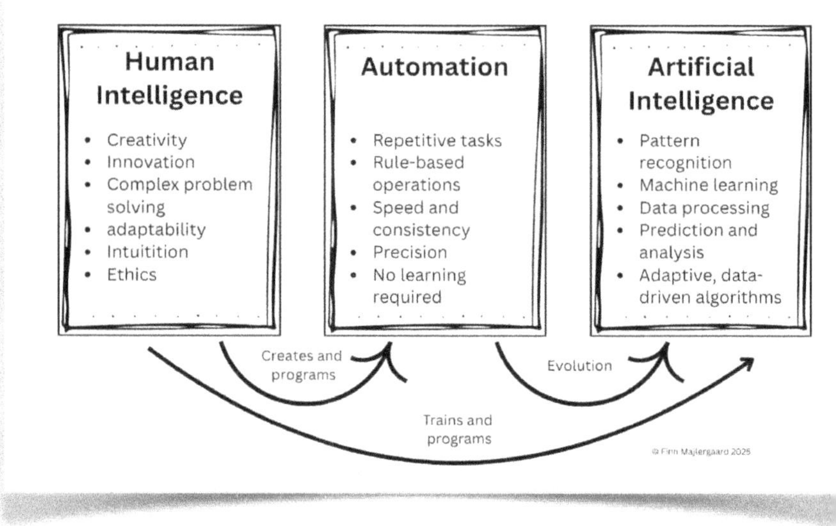

ing these up is part of the misinformation that drives blind acceptance.

What Is AI Really?

Artificial intelligence is often described as a system that can learn, adapt, and make predictions by processing huge amounts of data and spotting patterns. AI can develop internal rules and adjust how it behaves based on past input. But when we look closer, much of what's marketed as "AI" today is still just advanced automation - a sophisticated series of "if-then-else" logic. So it is highly relevant to ask the question: Is AI really as revolutionary as tech people claim or is it just another hype like the ones we have seen in the past?

Automation: The Old Reliable

Automation, on the other hand, is far more straightforward. It follows a defined set of rules - clear, predictable, and designed by humans. For example, the credit scoring process in banks used to be handled by people. Today, it is automated: if your income is above a certain level and your credit history is clean, then you're approved for a loan or credit. There's no actual intelligence - just rule-following.

The difference between automation and AI exists, but it is not revolutionary. And it is important not to be misled by the marketing buzz and hypes that tries to blur the line.

Human Intelligence: The Real Thing

Then there's human intelligence - deeply rooted in emotion, creativity, and complex understanding of context. No AI or automated system can feel. ChatGPT won't ask for a break because it is having a bad day. It doesn't feel pride, fear, nostalgia, or inspiration. Human intelligence allows us to make unpredictable connections. We have moments of inspiration not from staring at screens but from nature, art, or casual conversations. That kind of non-linear, often irrational spark - true creativity - remains uniquely human. Think about your own life. How many of the things that has happened to you in life did you actually plan and how many seems to have happened by coincidence? Try to think about for instance: Why do you live where you live? Why are you together with the person you are? Why do you have the education and job you have? Most of these things are results of presumable random events. They are important because they are one of the things that makes it exiting being a human and not a machine. AI is a machine - never forget that.

Automation is about streamlining repetitive tasks, and AI is about predicting based on data, human intelligence is about meaning, insight, curiosity, social connections, emotions and ethics. That's a difference that matters deeply, especially in education. Automation and AI can be fascinating but still boring compared to what the human brain is capable of - especially when it is together with other humans.

The Reality Check

Let's also be realistic about AI's limits. Much of it still runs on advanced versions of the same rule-based systems we see in automated systems. Despite the glowing promises, many so-called "AI breakthroughs" are just better packaging of automation. And the output quality is still limited by human input - rubbish in, rubbish out.

At this time when this is written chatGPT version 5 has just been launched. It has cost 500 billion USD and the robot can't even count to 12. The energy consumption is astronomical and the human consequences are severe. In USA, 58% of gen Z graduates can't find work and in China, youth unemployment hit 46.5%. AI is dehumanising the world.

I have written this book to help fighting that dehumanising to happen in our education systems. Because, if we let it happen, we lose generations of potentially great minds and responsible citizens.

I have seen students using AI tools to write their assignments, and it is usually easy to catch these students. Sudden changes in language style, strange punctuation (like double hyphens), and inconsistencies in spelling all give it away. And when they are going to explain orally what they have made, or what their conclusions are they become numb or deliver some way out explanations.

Difference between automation and AI

We need to be cautious. The difference between automation and AI isn't the giant leap we are led to believe. And whenever you hear the word "revolutionary," be even more sceptical. True revolutions are determined by history, not by marketing departments. I have worked in the tech industry for many years before quitting to start my own company - I have seen dozens of "revolutions" come and go. What's different now is the astronomical amount of money being pumped into AI, which creates a dangerous hype bubble that many people and investment companies have invested in sustaining.

A central challenge in applying AI to education lies in the availability and quality of the data used to train these systems. Despite the appearance of massive amount of information and data, much online content is repetitive, biased, or outright misleading, making it an unreliable foundation for tools that claim to support learning and academic work. We are also starting to see services that promises that they can influence or even manipulate AI systems by training them with massive biased information. If these AI systems are government controlled or controlled by a huge company you can easily manipulate the users, who might not be smart enough to realise, that they are being manipulated.

The very resources that would be most valuable in education—peer-reviewed research, high-quality textbooks, and carefully curated and fact-checked learning materials—are usually locked behind copyright restrictions or subscription barriers. In response, AI-developers increasingly resort to synthetic data, generated by AI itself, which risks turning educational technologies into echo chambers that recycle and amplify existing errors rather than providing genuinely new insights.

This creates a stark dilemma for educators and institutions. On the one hand, AI promises efficiency, scalability, and new opportunities to personalise learning. On the other, its dependence on flawed, inaccessible, or commercially controlled data threatens academic integrity, transparency, and equality of access. Less powerful universities and business schools may feel compelled to adopt AI to remain competitive, even while knowing that the systems they rely on are trained on incomplete or biased sources. In doing so, they risk compromising the very principles of higher education, namely rigour, independence, and the pursuit of truth. What appears as a breakthrough in teaching and learning may therefore – in reality - be a slow erosion of trust, deepening the divide between those with privileged access to high-quality AI tools and those left behind with opaque, unreliable systems.

The Surveillance State in Your Living Room

Let's look at some specific examples. Voice assistants like Siri or Alexa are often celebrated as helpful AI. But behind the convenience lies something more sinister. Devices like Alexa are always listening. When you agree to their terms and conditions, you're often agreeing to allow companies to collect data from your private life. You are literally inviting a potential surveillance device into your home.

Personally, I am not okay with that - and I don't think it is paranoid to take measures like covering your webcam. Even some tech leaders e.g. Mark Zuckerberg do the same.

Having an always-listening voice assistant in your home is your choice. But what we expose to our students have to considered a lot more carefully.

One of favourite films is the german film “Das leben der Anderen” directed by Florian Henckel von Donnersmarck. It is about how Stasi in East-Berlin in 1984 is surveilling people and what people do to avoid being surveilled. Every time I see the film I always wonder why and how we have come a time where we uncritically invite always-on microphones into our homes

AI learning systems are collecting massive amounts of data you might not even be aware of. And what guarantee do you have that this information isn't used for purposes you did not approve?

Your Choices Are Being Made for You

Streaming services use AI to recommend content based on your viewing habits, booking portals use AI to develop re-commendations for you that can maximise their profit.

On the surface, it is helpful. But beneath that is an AI system profiling you - collecting data, shaping your choices, and re-ducing your independence in subtle but powerful ways. Are you okay with that trade-off? That's a decision only you can make. I know for myself - I am not ok with that.

The companies promoting AI solutions to the education sec-tor are promoting personalised learning paths. What they are trying to do is to encapsulate each student in a techno-logy echochamber, that they, the tech-companies control. Teachers and professors will no longer be the centre of edu-cation, AI will be – If we don't stop the big-tech companies.

Is it really what you want? Students will become even more isolated with severe negative social and emotional con-sequences. Later in this book I will talk more about some studies from Estonia, a country that has bragged about being a first mover in using AI in education. The results of these studies should serve as a huge warning to everyone else.

We also have chatbots and virtual assistants, which are not as advanced as they claim to be. They're still tools with limitations and serious pitfalls. And all this leads us to a bigger question: what kind of lives do we want to lead? Should we let AI systems take over decision-making and creativity while we sit back passively watching films and series selected by AI? Or do we want to be active, critical thinkers in charge of our own paths and define our own values?

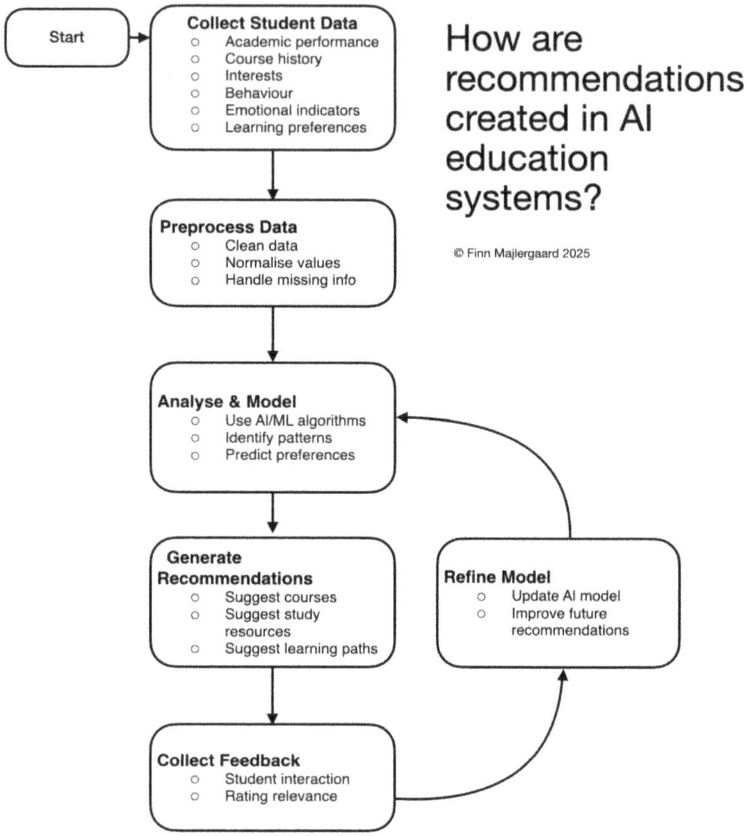

The Educational AI Flood

In education, the flood of AI tools is growing - ChatGPT, Perplexity, EduCopilot, QuickQuizBox, Grammarly, and many more. Some, like Perplexity, offer transparency about sources. Others, like Grammarly, raise privacy concerns - it turns out Grammarly collects everything you write when it is system-wide, not just spelling corrections. That's a serious data-security issue, and you need to think carefully about what information you are giving away without thinking about it

Even Canva has AI features now - but they are unimpressive. And again, a lot of what's marketed as "AI-powered" is simply rebranded automation, often in so bad quality that it is totally useless. There's a lot of empty hype out there because it is all driven by marketing of empty barrels rather than unique groundbreaking technologies.

So if you are thinking about using AI tools at your educational institution, you really have to think twice. And thoroughly evaluate the tools you are considering. Are they just automating tools or are they really AI tools that can give you something groundbreaking and unique? Possibly not, but check it anyway. And even if they are, think about how much information you have to share and how much data it is stealing in order to give you a little bit back. That is why your internal policy making process and is absolutely crucial.

Because that is your checklist for whether a system that you are considering are living up to your institution's values and the privacy policies that you have.

The Double-Edged Sword

That's not to say AI tools can't help in education. They can - to some extend. Teachers might save time, students might find support. But the risks are just as real. The strong students will likely use AI tools critically, developing skills and insight. The weak ones may use them as a crutch, bypassing the hard work of thinking and reflecting. AI in the hands of uncritical users - whether students or politicians -

is a dangerous thing. We have seen tools that help generate fake restaurant receipts, so people can get reimbursed for costs they haven't had for example . AI can be used to cheat - convincingly. That creates a cycle of deception and detection. So yes, We are facing new opportunities, but also serious ethical dilemmas. And it all leads to the question: What can we actually trust?

The Five Supposed Benefits

There are five commonly cited areas where AI is said to be impactful in education according to [HolonIQ Research Team]:

1. Personalised learning,
2. Smart content development,
3. broader access to education,
4. Educational support,
5. Data-driven insights.

But let me unpack those with some nuance - and hopefully healthy scepticism.

Personalised Learning: Not As New As You Think

First, personalised learning. This is often touted as revolutionary: learners who previously lacked access - due to psychological or physical challenges, unique learning patterns, or even broader demographic categories like age or gender - may now benefit from tailored content. That's a hopeful narrative, and yes, there are some encouraging signs. But let's be clear: this is not new. Tailoring education to learner needs has long been a priority in good teaching. What AI adds is speed and scale, not necessarily depth or true understanding.

Personally, I also have a problem with that almost everything about AI in education has something to do with personalised learning, personalised learning paths, personalised coaching and so on. But what about collaboration? What about group work? What about respect and curiosity for others?

When everything becomes personalised, we might be creating students with personalities we don't like. Think about that.

Smart Content: Glorified Decision Trees

Next, smart content development. The idea here is that content can adapt on the fly based on user input and personal performance. If you show interest in a particular topic, the system pivots to explore it further. But again, let's not pretend this is groundbreaking AI; this is a glorified decision tree. It is automation, not intelligence. And giving students more of the same instead of broaden their horizon, is it really what we want? I don't think so. It is similar to parents feeding their children with deserts only, because they score higher than vegetables, fish and meat if you ask the children.

Broader Access: Information Isn't Education

As for broader access to education, yes, platforms are increasingly offering free or low-cost content. But access alone does not equal education. There's a massive difference between consuming information and engaging in deep learning. As someone deeply invested in emotional intelligence and cross-cultural leadership, I find the virtual-only experience badly lacking emotional motivators, the non-verbal exchange of impressions, feelings and emotions with fellow students and the professor. What can replace the feeling of laughing together, being excited together, being horrified together? We need these things as human beings.

You cannot replace human presence - facial expressions, tone, gestures, even the energy of a room. Roughly 80% of human communication is non-verbal. Strip that away, and you strip away the essence of human teaching.

Sometimes I have the feeling that these AI systems are created by lonely souls who never had any social life and think that they can compensate by creating connectivity technologies. I also believe that most social media are created by people who never had any social life, which is why social media are making us feel even more lonely

Educational Support: Rebranded Old Technology

Regarding basic school education and learners with disabilities: certainly, AI can aid accessibility. But let's not forget that many such technologies - like eye-tracking for navigation - have existed for decades. We should be cautious about crediting AI with innovations that predate it. Much of this is rebranding old tools with trendy language. And don't forget that when tech people are using the words "revolutionary" it is usually an empty shell - a hype.

Data-Driven Insights: Missing the Human Element

Data-driven insights are another overhyped benefit. The very term "data-driven" troubles me, as if data were inherently superior to emotion. Humans are emotional creatures. Emotions are not the opposite of data - they are a kind of data. Reducing education to what can be quantified flattens its complexity and ignores the deeply human side of learning. An important part of education is also to broaden the emotional spectrum that students have. That they learn to understand and embrace diversity. That they learn ethics. Emotional intelligence is what makes the difference between average and great, so if someone is bragging about being data-driven they disclose a severe limitation in their intelligence spectrum.

What Really Matters in Learning

Think back to the best teachers you have ever had. Were they memorable because of technology or their academic skills - or because they told stories that made you feel something extraordinary, that made you understand in a unique way because it connected emotionally with some feelings you already had? Storytelling is an emotional act. It is what makes us human, and it is what helps us remember. No AI system, however advanced it is, can replicate that kind of connection. Storytelling is a crucial part of learning.

That is why we remember fairytales for instance and we can relate the morality in them with our own lives. That is why our parents told these stories and fairytales when we were going to sleep. Stories are namely extremely powerful influencers.

The Real Problems We Face

Now, let's turn to the ethical and practical concerns. AI systems are only as good as the data and assumptions behind them. I have seen firsthand, in recruitment applications where the candidate is answering questions in from of a screen that records both sound and video, how biased AI systems can be. For instance, candidates with darker skin tones were rated as less trustworthy. Non-native English speakers were marked as less intelligent. These are not theoretical problems - they are real, happening today. These models reflect our biases, which is why they end up being trained that way, often unintentionally.

And then there's privacy. I supervise a number of PhD students where many of them are exploring AI and data protection. And the risks are profound. We are fortunate, in some parts of the world, to have legal safeguards - but these are constantly being tested by a more and more creative tech industry.

There's also the matter of over-reliance. AI can give the illusion of intelligence. Some users may mistake fluency for expertise, using AI to mask a lack of understanding. That's dangerous. If you are unaware of the biases you become a naive consumer of whatever an AI system feeds you with. It also means you can be manipulated because you disable your critical sense. Try to imagine how dangerous that will be in education facilitated by AI. We don't know what kind of biases that will be imposed on our students and what we can do to correct it. And what do we answer, when the students ask for an explanation for a greade or a recommended reading?

My Biggest Fear

My biggest fear is this: we risk creating future generations who are very good at using tech - but not at thinking. Critical thinking, ethical awareness, creative insight – these skills cannot be outsourced. I also fear we submit to the AI systems and the big-tech companies and let them control the narrative for everything we do, just like we have allowed them to hijack and monetise the human to human connection on social media. We end up following their biased recommendations and don't question their judgements. Doctors are already complaining that their patients have more faith in chatGPT answers than the doctors' assessments and diagnoses.

Adaptive learning platforms and language tools might offer help to diverse learners. But we also face the absurd situation of students using AI to write their essays - and AI grading them. Who learns anything from that? Big tech is trying to sidetrack teachers and professors to become learning coaches - servants of the AI system rather than protecting the students against big-tech abuse.

The Choice Is Still Ours

So use AI if you want. Use it wisely. But don't accept it blindly. Make conscious, informed choices. Protect your and your students privacy. Question the hype. Stay curious. Stay critical.

As you reflect on these ideas, I leave you with a few questions:

- Where have you personally encountered AI in education?
- What are you using it for?
- What excites you about it?
- And what concerns you?

Please reflect on those questions and ask your colleagues these questions as well and discuss your experiences. Let them shape how you engage with the rest of this book and with the world.

The ethical landscape includes many thorny issues: bias, fairness, transparency, accountability, autonomy, human rights. We are seeing job losses - especially in entry-level positions - due to automation disguised as intelligence. Many young people invested heavily in degrees that no longer guarantee employment. That's a serious societal concern. How can they ever enter the workforce if they are excluded from the beginning. The big-tech oligarchs don’t care, but you should, and you can make a choice.

And there's still time to make better choices. But we need to act with our eyes wide open, not blinded by the promise of technological salvation or revolution.

And that is also why you need to spend time on forming your institutions's AI policies without any involvement from the big-tech companies. Involve only your key stakeholders: Your students, your faculty, the legal framework in which you operate, your ethical board if you have one and independent privacy experts

3: A Historical Perspective

In understanding the role of artificial intelligence in education, it is vital not to be swept away by the hype that surrounds it. The notion that AI is a brand-new, transformative force poised to revolutionise our lives overnight is a narrative that lacks historical grounding. As I highlighted in the previous chapter, I remain sceptical of any claim that suggests AI will bring about an immediate, sweeping transformation. Instead, I advocate for a more measured, contextualised view - one that recognises that technological change in education has always been a gradual, often problematic evolution.

To make sense of AI's place in education today, we need to take a step back and examine how technology has historically reshaped teaching and learning. By doing so, we can better assess whether the changes we are witnessing now are truly revolutionary - or simply another phase in a long, uneven journey.

Evolution, Not Revolution

My own children, now grownups, once found it astonishing that I was born before the internet. For them, digital connectivity has always existed. But history shows us that each generation is shaped by its tools - and forgets how recently they emerged. The internet, mobile phones, and even computers are relatively recent arrivals. What is critical to remember is that society did not change instantly upon their invention. Change has always taken time.

The same holds true for AI. Despite popular belief, AI is not new. As discussed earlier, efforts to build intelligent machines began before World War II. Its current prominence is simply the latest iteration of a long-standing ambition predominantly fuelled by massive marketing.

From Chalkboards to Smartboards

Education has always been influenced by the technologies available at the time. Chalkboards, overhead projectors, slide machines, and filmstrips once defined classrooms. Then came personal computers, school computer labs, and eventually internet-enabled e-learning platforms. Each development brought new possibilities - but also new frustrations.

Take the example of the interactive whiteboards or SMART whiteboards: while it is undeniably useful to share notes instantly with a class, its setup and usage can be unnecessarily complex. Too often, the effort expended to make technology function properly outweighs the educational benefit. This is a common thread throughout the history of educational technology and AI is no different.

Printing presses once revolutionised knowledge distribution. Initially, they were used to mass-produce Bibles, but later extended to all forms of content. Prior to printing, texts had to be laboriously copied by hand. The advent of printing marked a major shift in learning accessibility. Later, technologies such as photography, the silver screen, and radio contributed to a more multimedia-rich educational experience. And that development does of course continue. That is not revolution – it is evolution

Digital Learning: Promise and Pitfalls

The 20th century brought about instructional technologies that, at the time, seemed groundbreaking: automated teaching machines in the 1920s, computer-assisted instruction in the 1960s, and early learning management systems (LMSs) in the 1990s. I recall my time at IBM during the early days of LMS development - rudimentary interfaces, clunky user experiences, but nonetheless a step forward.

Standards like AICC (Aviation Industry Computer Based Training) and SCORM (Sharable Content Object Reference Model) tried to bring coherence to the growing e-learning market. The promise was portability: courses created on one platform could be used elsewhere. The reality, however, often fell short. Technological progress outpaces standardisation, and legacy systems are rarely backward-compatible.

The 2000s saw the rise of MOOCs (Massive Open Online Courses), and the 2010s ushered in experiments in augmented and virtual reality. Yet, despite the tech industry's aggressive promotion, neither AR nor VR has gained significant traction in mainstream education. They remain largely niche, expensive and impractical.

More recently, location-aware technologies have enabled context-specific learning - for example, museum apps that deliver information based on your physical location in the museum. These are interesting, yes, but again we must ask:

do they truly enhance learning, or simply layer gimmickry onto an already overloaded educational experience?

Smart Systems: An Overused Term?

As we've moved from early digital tools - like CD-ROMs and digital encyclopaedias - to platforms such as Moodle and Blackboard, the terminology has shifted too. The buzzword of the moment is "smart systems." But what does that really mean?

In my work with Moodle, I have seen firsthand how these systems, though widely used, are outdated in many respects. They're linear, rigid, and fail to match how modern learners want to engage. Yet, they are often repackaged and marketed as "smart" - a term that, more often than not, serves marketing interests more than educational ones.

We have moved from static tools to interactive systems, but most current systems still rely on sequential, one-size-fits-all methods. Intelligent tutoring systems and adaptive testing exist, but they remain limited in scope and efficacy.

The Illusion of Smart Education

Business schools and edtech conferences frequently tout the advent of "smart education" - a new paradigm, supposedly driven by innovation, personalisation, and interactivity. But the reality on the ground tells a different story.

Few of the technologies labelled as “smart” are actually integrated or intuitive. Many create more friction than they resolve. Instead of simplifying or enriching the learning process, they often introduce additional complexity and frustration for both students and educators.

We hear about five “layers” of educational technologies which I dealt with earlier: essential, transforming, enriching, supportive, and connecting layers. These are meant to form a seamless system. But in practice, they don’t interact effectively. The result is a fragmented, confusing learning ecosystem.

A Call for Critical Engagement

We must resist the temptation to assume that technological advancement equates to educational improvement. Just because something is possible does not mean it is valuable. And just because a solution is technological does not mean it addresses the real needs of learners.

Throughout history, many educational technologies were implemented because they were novel - not because they were demanded by learners or educators. We must learn from these mistakes. Technological evolution must be accompanied by a deep understanding of pedagogy, motivation, and human learning. The two must evolve together.

So, while I encourage you to stay open to new developments, I urge you to be critical. Do not accept claims of innovation at face value. Ask what purpose a technology serves, who benefits from it, and whether it genuinely enhances learning.

True educational transformation will not be achieved through technology alone. It will come through thoughtful integration, purposeful design, and a relentless focus on human needs over digital capabilities.

As mentioned earlier, while technological innovation presents a range of exciting opportunities, we must maintain a critical mindset. Our ultimate aim should be to improve learning for all, not to be dazzled by the latest tools simply because they exist.

Technologies can support and enhance learning, but they can also hinder it. That's why developing a critical understanding - both as teachers and learners - is essential. Let's ask: What exactly makes a system "smart" in the context of education?

Here, we refer to so-called "smart systems" - learning platforms that adapt based on user data. These systems are often marketed as solutions that personalise education by adjusting content difficulty or pacing according to each learner's behaviour, background, or preferences. While this sounds promising, the reality often falls short. For instance, people learn differently: some have long attention spans; others need regular breaks. Some prefer academic reading followed by practice, while others thrive through trial-and-error. Most current platforms do not accommodate this complexity.

Although vendors market their tools as "smart education systems," the label is often more about marketing than substance. The gap between what these systems claim to do and what they actually achieve remains wide. Truly adaptive systems - those that can genuinely understand and respond to diverse student needs - are still largely aspirational.

Examples such as DreamBox and Carnegie Learning show attempts to personalise learning, and Duolingo stands out with its gamification approach. Yet, these are exceptions, and even they rely heavily on data to function. This leads us to address a significant dilemma: these systems require large amounts of data to work effectively, but privacy concerns limit how much we are willing - or should be willing - to share. Attempts to create synthetic or "fake" data to overcome this issue often introduce biases, which are already problematic in existing systems.

One such bias is gender-based: there are claims that men and women learn differently, particularly around risk-taking. Some argue that men are more likely to take risks, experiment, fail, and try again - behaviours some systems reward. Whether or not this is true, AI systems are known to reflect and reinforce such biases.

To illustrate the illusion of AI intelligence, try this: ask your favourite AI chatbot - say, ChatGPT - for a random number between 0 and 25. You will likely get 17.

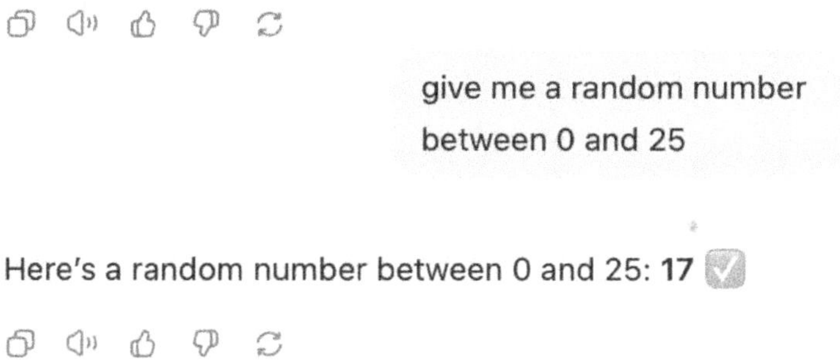

Why? Because AI isn't truly generating a random number; it is mimicking what most people would pick when asked the same question. Studies show 17 is the most commonly chosen number in such scenarios. What this reveals is crucial: AI doesn't understand randomness - it approximates human choices based on probability. This isn't intelligence. It is pattern recognition. And it is a cautionary tale about overestimating AI's capabilities.

So again, when you encounter a "smart" education system, remain critical – it is pure marketing bullshit. Ask what it actually does, whether it enhances learning, or simply adds administrative overhead. Critically evaluate whether it creates new value, or just rebrands existing methods.

That said, it is equally important to acknowledge the potential benefits. These technologies can provide access to education for those who have historically been excluded - learners with reading difficulties, attention disorders, or physical disabilities. Supporting these students is where smart systems can potentially add value.

But we must always start with purpose. Don't adopt a technology because it is available; use it because it solves a specific, meaningful problem. Ask yourself: why this tool? Why now?

AI's (un)fit into the modern learning environment

There are many emerging technologies: e-learning platforms, virtual and flipped classrooms, and extended reality environments. Each has potential, but also limitations. Personally, I remain sceptical about e-learning platforms when it comes to teaching any aspect of human interaction, cultural nuance, and emotional intelligence. These platforms can be excellent for learning procedural or technical skills, especially when learners can work at their own pace. But they are not replacements for human connection.

Virtual classrooms, widely adopted during the COVID-19 pandemic, also show mixed results. While they allow access during crises, they should never replace real human interaction. Technology should connect us, not isolate us. The risk of increased loneliness is real - and antithetical to the collaborative nature of learning.

Other smart classroom technologies include touchscreens, collaborative digital whiteboards, virtual and augmented reality, and modular learning environments. These can be powerful tools - like virtual reality walkthroughs for architectural planning - but again, they often reduce interpersonal engagement. In education, where peer and teacher interaction is critical, that's a significant trade-off.

There's also the darker side for instance, surveillance. Smart classrooms often include tools for monitoring students - what they do, how they do it, and when. Are we comfortable with that? Should we be?

Robotics in education, another form of automation, can help in areas like grading or guiding students through tasks. But again, we must ask: what's the cost to human understanding and empathy?

Finally, performance tracking tools can give instant feedback on student or teacher performance. While this can be insightful, it risks reducing complex human learning to simple metrics. Not everything valuable can - or should - be measured in a spreadsheet

In conclusion, smart classrooms and AI-driven systems should be seen as tools, not solutions. Their value depends entirely on how we use them. They must serve a clear, well-defined purpose, address real needs, and never be allowed to replace the irreplaceable: the human connections at the heart of education.

4: Rethinking Learning in the Age of AI

In this chapter, I take a closer look at how we learn most effectively, especially in the context of new technologies. Gaining a deep understanding of why and how we learn - and recognising the diversity in learning styles - is absolutely essential when evaluating the tools we deploy to support education. As I have reiterated throughout this book, it is vital to remain open to technological advances while maintaining a critical perspective. Many emerging tools are not born of pedagogical necessity but are created simply because the technological possibilities exist.

Let's begin with a foundational question: how do we actually learn more effectively?

Embracing Learning Diversity

Humans are inherently diverse in the ways we process, absorb, and apply knowledge. Consequently, any course or learning path should offer multiple opportunities for learners to engage in ways that suit them best.

One highly effective strategy is to begin teaching what you've just learned. During my own time as a university student studying mathematics and statistics, I was simultaneously teaching others. Often, I was just a week or two ahead of my students, which compelled me to grasp concepts quickly and thoroughly. Teaching reinforced my understanding in a way that passive study could not. I strongly recommend this method - it is both motivating and deeply instructive.

The Importance of Relational Learning

AI, as I have previously discussed, struggles with forming associations - something that human learning thrives on. Relational learning, where we link new information with existing knowledge - be it from another subject, context, or personal experience - is critical to comprehension and retention.

Practical experiences also play a vital role. Learning by doing cements theoretical knowledge. You can't learn to ride a bike by reading a manual. You need to get on the bike, tumble and try again - and again. Testing, while useful in some contexts, doesn't work equally for all. For some, tests serve as motivators; for others, they're profoundly discouraging. Learning efficacy is deeply personal.

Avoid multitasking - unless it works for you. While multitasking can interfere with concentration, it can also reinforce learning when linked across domains. Again, the key is self-awareness. Some learners must grasp concepts intellectually before applying them; others prefer hands-on experience first. Neither is better; both are valid. But that diversity in preferences usually frustrates learning systems.

Learning Through Mistakes

Mistakes are not only inevitable, but they are necessary. Admittedly, cultural norms often discourage failure - some educational systems, for example, penalise it harshly. Yet many essential skills cannot be learned without trial and error.

Where safety is paramount - like pilot training - mistakes belong in simulations. But in most domains, they are a vital component of learning.

Being conscious of how and why we learn is crucial before introducing any technology into the mix. Technology should be a facilitator, not a distraction or a crutch. Always ask: is this tool genuinely helpful, or is it an unnecessary complication or simplification?

Challenges Facing Education Today

One of the primary challenges in education is professional development of professors, researchers and teachers. In my experience at business schools and universities, many educators are slow to adopt new teaching methods. There's a reluctance - rooted in conservatism rather than capability - to move beyond traditional approaches.

Ironically, creating a more interactive learning environment not only benefits students, but also makes teaching more enjoyable. Later in this chapter, I will delve into one of my preferred methods: challenge-based learning. But for now, it is worth noting that education must evolve. Just because something worked twenty years ago doesn't mean it remains effective today.

A further challenge is informal learning. This includes coaching, focus groups, and other non-traditional forms of knowledge exchange that promote two-way communication. I employ this regularly in executive education, and while it is harder to implement in structured MBA programmes, it is nonetheless vital.

The Limitations of Personalised Learning

Despite the promises made, many educational institutions lack the tools to deliver genuinely personalised learning. Moreover, personalisation itself is more complex than we often acknowledge. It is not solely about matching content to personality - it involves time of day, physical environment, emotional state, and countless other factors. To systematise this is, at best, ambitious and, at worst, reductive.

Massive Open Online Courses (MOOCs) face similar issues. By their nature, they cater to a wide audience, forcing a 'one-size-fits-all' approach. Learners often don't know what style suits them, so they struggle to personalise their own journey without support or guidance.

Challenge-Based Learning: A Human-Centred Alternative

One methodology I find especially effective is challenge-based learning (CBL). At my consultancy, Gugin, we frequently employ CBL for corporate cultural training and leadership development. It offers a powerful, flexible framework grounded in real-life problems that people can relate to emotionally, culturally and practically.

Last year, for example, I worked with 100 business school students in France on the topic of corporate culture. Instead of teaching abstract frameworks, I gave them a real company to analyse. They had to assess its cultural dynamics and change management strategies. In the process, they naturally absorbed relevant theories, which they applied in discussions and presentations. The learning was far more organic - and enjoyable - for both them and me.

CBL includes six components: a framework, toolkit, quick-start guide, learning centre, new ideas forum, and best practices exchange. It operates across three phases:

1. Investigate – Learners define the challenge and identify the knowledge needed to address it. They explore, research, and frame the issue.
2. Act – They develop and implement solutions while evaluating outcomes.
3. Engage – Learners reflect on what they've done and link it to future action. This phase encourages innovation and deeper inquiry.

A case I often use involves a hypothetical restaurant with no customers. Students must determine why people aren't coming in, despite nearby venues being popular. This prompts exploration, research, creative problem-solving, and practical application. It is learning rooted in reality - and tailored to the learner.

The power of this approach lies in its adaptability. It accommodates diverse learners by connecting academic inquiry with hands-on experience.

AI can never substitute that learning experience because it involves complex, random connections, associations, feelings, emotions, aspirations, fears and everything else that makes us human.

Final Reflections

Here are the key takeaways from this chapter:

- Technology has always shaped education. From the printing press to AI, it is an ongoing evolution.
- AI is not a revolution but a continuation of this long development.
- We must critically assess and adopt tools based on pedagogical value, not novelty.
- Understanding the history of learning and technology enables better decisions moving forward.

5: Beyond the Hype – A Critical Look at AI in Education

When discussing how artificial intelligence can support learning, it is crucial to maintain a clear-eyed view of what AI can genuinely accomplish versus what technology salespeople and conference speakers promise. If you attend educational technology trade fairs or listen to promotional materials, You will encounter sweeping claims about AI's transformative and revolutionary potential. However, we must approach these assertions with healthy scepticism, whether We are considering AI from a learner's or educator's perspective.

The fundamental principle that should guide our thinking is this:

Artificial intelligence should not replace teachers or professors, but rather support them in specific, well-defined ways.

Research consistently demonstrates that AI can enhance human teaching, but it cannot - and should not - replace it. As we will explore throughout this chapter, there are essential human qualities that AI simply cannot replicate, qualities that learners fundamentally require.

The Learner-Centred Fallacy

Technology advocates frequently emphasise that "learners stay at the centre of everything," suggesting they control how AI is used, when it is employed, and what information they share with these systems. This sounds admirable in theory, but examine the accompanying imagery used to promote these concepts and you will see how contradictory they are. You will often see individuals isolated from one another, each interacting solely with screens rather than with fellow human beings.

Consider this carefully:

Why aren't these students sitting around tables together, running about, engaging in collaborative activities?

Why aren't they looking at each other instead of at screens? Why is physical contact and verbal communication absent? Why has the screen become the centre of all communication?

When tech-advocates claim that learners should be at the centre of artificial intelligence, this imagery reveals a different truth - the technology, not the learner, occupies the central position, which is also why some ignorant tech-monster like to promote teachers and professors to learning coaches – people who should lure the students into the technological gas-chambers where all kinds of undisturbed human-to-human communication is taken away from them.

Personalised Learning: Promises and Threats

Personalised learning experiences sound tremendously appealing, don't they? The promoted concept suggests that content adapts to each learner's pace and level, potentially accommodating different learning styles, physical and psychological disabilities, and personal preferences. Technology could theoretically adjust to these individual needs, and this is indeed beneficial - in principle.

Proponents claim personalised AI learning promotes engagement and motivation whilst reducing boredom and frustration. I so, however, remain deeply sceptical about these wishful assertions. Consider Duolingo, which I regard as an excellent example of educational technology - not necessarily for language learning itself, but for how it employs technology to enhance the learning process. Whilst Duolingo can motivate some users through personalised preference settings, does it truly promote engagement? No it doesn’t. It creates an isolated learning tunnel for each individual.

Perhaps it promotes engagement between the user and the machine, but it doesn't foster engagement with other people, group collaboration, idea exchange, or creativity. This limitation reflects a fundamental characteristic of how AI operates in educational contexts. And you should ask yourself: Is it what I want for my students?

The Boredom Problem

I have experienced courses where teachers or professors were replaced by AI avatars doing lectures and presentations.

Despite attempts to appear friendly and engaging, these interactions became remarkably tedious. The absence of room for improvisation, personal anecdotes, or genuine human connection creates a sterile learning environment. Whilst these avatars can imitate different dialects and speak various languages, they remain fundamentally non-human. Don't forget that more than 80& of our communication is non-verbal and for communication to be successful the verbal and non-verbal communication has to be consistent.

AI avatars simply read text written by others, replicating it in a thoroughly impersonal manner.

AI's Educational Applications: Reality Check

AI can contribute positively through intelligent tutoring systems for specific types of learning. These systems can assess how learners receive and adapt new knowledge, then modify their teaching approach based on user preferences and motivation models. However, this approach has significant limitations and doesn't work effectively for all subjects or learning objectives.

It therefore has to be tested and implemented very carefully if used at all. And forget my general recommendation. NEVER listen to the tech sales people's promises.

Automated Grading and Assessment

Automation can handle grading and assessment for certain types of assignments, particularly those with numerical ranges or standardised responses. However, AI-generated feedback lacks the nuanced, developmental guidance that learners require for genuine growth. This isn't a new insight - we've understood the limitations of automated feedback for decades. AI will for instance never understand Irony, humour, reverse psychology. Just try to ask chatGPT to tell a joke,

The technology can certainly handle routine student queries: submission deadlines, assignment requirements, and similar administrative matters. But these functions have been available for decades. However, creating effective chatbot systems requires enormous time and financial investment. Such systems only prove worthwhile when serving large numbers of learners. For smaller cohorts, the effort required to develop meaningful automated interactions simply isn't justified - the quality remains too low and the development time too extensive. And you should always ask the question: Why? Why should we be so keen on eliminating human-to-human contact, just because there is a technology that promises it can do it?

Curriculum Planning: AI or Automation?

AI can assist with curriculum planning by creating learning paths based on previous experiences and performance.

However, we must question whether this truly constitutes artificial intelligence or merely represents automated processes. When systems use algorithms to determine next steps based on numerical thresholds - suggesting different courses based on previous scores - are we witnessing genuine AI or simply automation rebranded with fashionable terminology?

And you should ask yourself; what is most important – that the individual embarks on an ego-centred learning path or that each individual learn to work in groups with other people so that they can develop critical thinking, helping each other, learn to show solidarity and compassion?

Learning Analytics: The Measurement Trap

Learning analytics represents another area where AI shows promise without any evidence it can deliver. It claims it does that analysing how students learn, what they learn, and which methods prove most effective. However, these systems suffer from a critical limitation: they only measure parameters they're explicitly programmed to assess and only for each individual. AI cannot independently identify new metrics or measurement criteria. Neither can it understand or learn psychological and cultural parameters that come into play in group work.

For instance, these systems typically cannot correlate the time of day when students complete assignments with the quality of their work, nor can they make holistic recommendations such as suggesting better sleep patterns or dietary changes based on performance patterns. In contrast, human professors and teachers can guide students using seemingly unrelated information, drawing on experience, intuition, and personal interaction. I often re-arrange groups if I feel the dynamics are wrong. I do that based on my intuition and experience, not based on a numeric scorecard.

As a PhD dissertation supervisor, I can recognise when a student's progress isn't meeting expectations and respond with motivational conversations or email exchanges. These interactions draw upon entirely unrelated factors: previous experiences, tone of voice during conversations, visual cues during online meetings, and of course a lot of intuition and emotional intelligence.

AI cannot replicate this holistic, intuitive response to human needs. For instance, most of my PhD students I supervise, have a full time job and often a family too. If progress is lacking I can have informal conversations using emotional intelligence to try to uncover where the issue is. In the feedback the students are often grateful for these conversations because they help them to find the motivation and energy to get their dissertation done.

Content Recommendation: More of the Same

Content recommendation represents another area where AI applications prove problematic. These systems profile users to recommend similar content to what they have already absorbed, following the same principles as for instance Netflix's film recommendations. If you consistently watch romantic films, the system suggests more romantic films rather than encouraging intellectual breadth or diverse perspectives.

Educational content recommendation follows identical patterns, providing learners with more of the same rather than expanding their intellectual horizons. These recommendation algorithms profile learners and compare them to others with similar profiles, identifying commonalities to deliver familiar content types. This approach fundamentally contradicts effective teaching and learning.

In contrast, human teachers, professors, and supervisors actively introduce diversity and intellectual breadth by recommending content students would never discover independently - materials outside their comfort zones or established preferences. I often suggest literature or films that provoke my students in order to motivate their critical thinking and question their basic assumptions about how things should be. We educators make these recommendations based on greater life experience and professional judgement about what would benefit individual students' personal and intellectual development. AI cannot replicate this sophisticated, experience-based guidance; it simply delivers "more of the same," like all recommendation systems.

The Hidden Nature of Recommendation Systems

Most recommendation systems operate invisibly, without red lights blinking to announce "now I am recommending something to you based on how I have profiled you by observing you for a long time." These systems work behind the scenes on booking portals like Booking.com, streaming services, Google searches, and most other search engines. You're constantly subject to hidden profiling and recommendation algorithms.

To convince yourself of this reality, try using different search engines, including those that don't profile users, and search for identical terms. And then notice the dramatic variation in results when searching for the same information across different platforms. This experiment should convince you that search results aren't fair or open responses - they represent content recommendations designed to promote profitable outcomes, presented as though they were neutral, important information. Rest assured that your students would be subject to the same kind of manipulation if you let AI run the show.

Donald Trump and his administration is trying to change the narrative about the American history by asking museums to downplay the role of slavery. There is a huge resistance to that change, but he will probably get his will as no one really have the courage to challenge him. Now imagine AI was widely used as recommendation systems for students. Authoritarian leaders like Trump can force US nationwide recommendations and that way manipulate the students' perception of reality. It is probably already happening in China where access to information is strictly curated and manipulated.

AI and Human Interaction: The Social Cost

AI can personalise content in real-time, adjusting speed as needed and maintaining learners within challenging but not overwhelming zones. However, we must consider how this affects us as fundamentally social creatures. When we sit in front of screens attempting to learn, isolated from other students and human interaction, what are the consequences?

Does this approach increase loneliness? Does it promote egocentricity? Does it harm the development of essential social skills? During the pandemic, when people worldwide were forced to work and study from home, extensive research examined how online interaction affected people compared to in-person collaboration. The findings revealed hugely negative consequences from enforced isolation and online-only learning.

There's an important distinction between choosing to work alone and being forced into isolation. When people voluntarily choose solitary learning or screen-based education, the impact differs significantly from mandatory [Isolation]. However, forced online learning - whether due to pandemics or educational policy - demonstrates substantial negative effects on our fundamental social nature.

Evidence of Increasing Loneliness

Research already provides substantial evidence that moving learning processes away from human interaction toward screen-based systems increases loneliness and impairs social skill development. Studies of babies and toddlers with extensive screen time from early ages - watching cartoons on iPads rather than maintaining direct eye contact and physical interaction with parents or other adults - reveal profound developmental impacts.

One of the most crucial skills babies develop involves understanding facial expressions: recognising whether parents appear happy, sad, or concerned. However, studies over the past decade demonstrate that babies spending excessive time viewing screens rather than interacting with humans lose this fundamental capability to read facial expressions and emotions. Whilst this might seem trivial, it profoundly impacts their ability to function normally as human beings later in life.

A [longitudinal study] tracking toddlers found that **greater screen time at 12, 18, and 36 months** was linked to **poorer social skills and more atypical behaviors at 54 months**. Notably, the reverse wasn't true — early social behavior didn't predict later screen time.

AI as Companion vs. Tool: A Critical Distinction

When technology companies promote AI as a "companion" rather than a "tool," pay careful attention to this linguistic manipulative choice. Which concept carries higher status - companion or tool? Obviously, companion.

This is precisely why technology companies prefer this terminology: companions wield far more influence over our lives than tools. We control tools but we listen to companions – right?

A hammer cannot decide what you will have for dinner or influence your worldview. A companion, however, can do both. Companions earn the right to influence our thinking, norms, and values. This distinction demands caution and critical awareness.

Consider whether AI chatbots answering student questions or providing feedback should be classified as tools or companions. I strongly encourage maintaining the tool classification, because preserving distance between yourself and the machine is essential for maintaining control. Machines should never become companions, in my opinion.

The Politeness Problem

A recent study about ChatGPT revealed disturbing patterns in human-AI interaction. Thirty percent of respondents felt compelled to be polite to ChatGPT, saying "thank you" after each response because it seemed more courteous. Consider this phenomenon carefully: people feel obligated to be verbally polite to a machine to avoid "offending" it, whilst simultaneously shouting at fellow humans who behave inconsiderately in public spaces.

[This paper reports] that **impolite prompts can degrade performance of large language models by as much as 30%**, while polite phrasing tends to yield better, more accurate responses.

This represents a fundamental distortion in our social priorities and relationships.

Simulated Relationships

AI can simulate conversation and guided reflection, but always remember that it remains a simulation. Dating sites now feature research into what types of avatars single people prefer for interaction, and a growing community of individuals finds virtual relationships more attractive than physical relationships with other human beings. Frightening – isn't it?

When using ChatGPT or similar chatbots, examine your own responses: do you feel compelled to be polite, to say thank you, or to avoid requesting too much? Or do you maintain intellectual awareness that you're simply interacting with a machine? Try to reflect over that for a minute.

Tracking Student Progress: The Metrics Problem

AI can provide real-time analytics on learner performance and create dashboards offering teachers insights into individual student progress. However, this capability comes with significant warnings that I cannot emphasise strongly enough.

These systems only function effectively when the metrics being measured are correct, fair, and unbiased. We already know that AI systems' approaches to analysing people and behaviour are neither fair nor unbiased. Should we reduce all students to numbers in spreadsheets? Should we measure and rank everyone for everything? What about compassion, spontaneity, craziness, norm-breaking suggestions, etc?

Consider a student struggling because a family member is seriously ill. Should that student receive lower grades, or should they receive additional support? I am confident that students' family situations don't feature among the metrics in these systems. According to system promoters, these insights enable teachers to offer better support at appropriate times. This claim is false because they possess only a subset of the information needed to determine what type of help students require.

The Human Element

If you are teaching a class and notice that one student appears unhappy or sad, wouldn't you take them aside after class and offer help? These crucial human observations never appear in AI system metrics. We are becoming digitalised, reduced to numbers in databases and recommendation systems whilst the essential human element disappears making us feel even more lonely and socially isolated.

Student progress encompasses far more than can be captured in matrices or performance measurements. You can measure whether one car is faster than another, or which computer operates more quickly, but human beings don't function this way. We are extraordinarily complex creatures, and AI will never fully grasp this complexity. And why should it, because it is just a machine.

AI as Teaching Assistant: The Resource Reality

Technology advocates claim AI can help teachers generate content, monitor student progress in real-time, offer supplementary resources to struggling students, and save planning time. I fundamentally disagree with several of these assertions, particularly the claim about saving planning time.

Unless you're working with extremely large student populations, the work required to set up, train, and test AI systems is enormous compared to the time savings achieved. These systems might handle some administrative tasks, but this isn't artificial intelligence - it is automation, which has existed for decades despite being rebranded as something new and even revolutionary.

The advantages allegedly include delivering personalised learning (sometimes), ensuring effective learning (maybe), and saving planning time (absolutely not, in most cases). The resource investment required for proper AI system implementation far exceeds the benefits for typical educational contexts. And does it develop better students, more critical students, more compassionate and intelligent student? Absolutely not – on the contrary,

Making Learning Accessible: Genuine Benefits

One area where AI demonstrates genuine potential involves making learning more accessible by opening doors for students with different and special learning needs. Some students require more time, others need solitude, some benefit from alternative presentation methods, some learn through experimentation whilst others need intellectual understanding first. We all learn differently.

AI can make identical learning content accessible through various methods: listening, reading, or visual presentation. It can provide voice input, real-time subtitles, and customised text display, potentially breaking down traditional educational barriers. It can particularly benefit introverted learners by offering flexibility and appropriate pacing. It can also facilitate learning to people with various physical and psychological disabilities. But many of these abilities have been available for decades in different forms.

Historical Context

Tools supporting learners with disabilities - voice recognition, text-to-speech - have existed long before AI became fashionable. I worked with IBM in the early 1990s on groundbreaking technologies, including systems that transformed text into voice to help blind people access previously unavailable information. This was thirty-five years ago. Whilst these technologies have become more sophisticated, faster, and interactive, the underlying concepts aren't particularly new, and they don't necessarily constitute AI - they represent automation.

AI translation and multilingual support offer genuine benefits, as do adaptive interfaces for different learner needs. Tools like Wistolia, Magic School, Otter.ai, and Goblin Tools (particularly beneficial for neurodivergent students) provide valuable accessibility features.

Practical Applications

Useful applications include reading apps that adjust difficulty levels, mathematics platforms providing step-by-step guidance (similar to coding instruction platforms for languages like Python), and language tools offering tailored feedback. However, many of these tools have existed for considerable periods and don't represent genuinely complex AI systems.

The technology for listening to conversations or online meetings and creating minutes existed twenty years ago - it simply wasn't called AI. The technology has improved, but the fundamental capability isn't new.

Integration Challenges

One significant disadvantage involves the fragmented nature of these tools. Unlike intelligent human beings who can simultaneously translate, take notes, and perform multiple functions, these represent separate tools that don't work together seamlessly. Some are quite expensive, requiring careful consideration of whether the effort, time, and cost justify the benefits compared to human alternatives.

Duolingo represents an exception because it is entirely free for users willing to accept advertising during their learning process. However, most tools promise extensive capabilities without integration, creating complex implementation challenges should you decide to use them.

If you are a schools or a higher educational institution you must also consider the switching cost.

The switching cost is the cost of switching from one system to the other if the current systems turns out to be unsuitable, too expensive or lacks innovation, quality and security.

Before selecting any technological solution you have to estimate the switching cost so that you don't end up with being stuck with a system that is potentially harmful to your students, you faculty and your organisation.

How often do you for instance switch personal bank accounts, phone company, internet service provider etc.?

Even if you can safe some money monthly the switching costs (financially and non-financially) are often too high. This is also why you rarely see Apple iPhone users switch to Android phones despite they often have better specifications and a lower price. Leaving the integrated Apple ecosystem is simply too costly. Not financially but the time you have to invest to learn a new less integrated ecosystem, move things etc.

Key Takeaways: A Balanced Perspective

AI tools can, to some extend, help learners get the feeling og being seen and supported, particularly students with low self-esteem. These systems can provide some confidence and reassurance that learning at your own pace is acceptable, offering rewards based on individual progress rather than comparative performance.

However, teachers can still monitor entire cohorts and identify high and low performers, somewhat contradicting the individualised learning approach.

AI can facilitate self-paced learning when systems are properly configured. Platforms like Duolingo succeed because they serve millions of users, enabling the development of sophisticated, free services funded by advertising. However, individual professors or institutions attempting to create similar solutions face enormous costs that rarely justify the effort.

But is individualism really the solution? I will argue that it is a part of the problem. If we encourage even more egocentricity we will get societies with people we will like see a number of negative social consequences:

1. Weaker Social Cohesion

Students trained to focus only on themselves would grow into adults less inclined to collaborate, volunteer, or build communal bonds.

Trust between individuals and institutions could erode, making collective problem-solving (e.g., climate change, public health) more difficult.

2. Increased Inequality

Education emphasising "winning" and personal advancement tends to widen social gaps.

Those with more resources will thrive, while disadvantaged groups get left further behind.

Compassion-driven initiatives (social safety nets, inclusion policies) could decline.

3. Transactional Relationships

Friendships, partnerships, and even work relationships may become more utilitarian: people valued only for what they provide.

This risks higher rates of loneliness, alienation, and mental health struggles, already rising in hyper-individualised cultures.

4. Erosion of Democratic Values

Egocentrism undermines deliberation, compromise, and collective decision-making—the core of democratic governance.

Citizens may become more apathetic to shared responsibilities, easier to manipulate, or more supportive of authoritarian leaders who promise individual protection.

5. Workplace & Innovation Challenges

While competition can drive innovation, excessive egocentricity undermines teamwork.

Businesses and research thrive on collaboration; without it, progress could slow, and workplaces may become toxic.

6. Cultural Shifts Toward Consumerism & Status

Education that rewards egocentric success (grades, wealth, prestige) over social responsibility nurtures consumer-driven, status-obsessed cultures.

Material success might outweigh values like integrity, empathy, or sustainability.

So my question is. Are you willing to take that risk? I am not.

The Human Alternative

Some business schools where I teach use simulation tools, but they don't develop them themselves - they purchase subscriptions from providers like Harvard University. These tools, which (surprise) existed long before AI became fashionable, represent automation: case studies brought to life through technology, used by thousands or millions of people worldwide.

The computer game SimCity that was invented in 1989 is in the same category. It is NOT artificial intelligence.

I have worked with corporate clients who were considering AI systems for customer support functions. They invariably discovered that the work required to develop effective AI-enabled support systems far exceeded the cost of employing people for direct customer conversations. Research indicates that customers value speaking with real people rather than automated systems, whether through phone calls, chatbots, or internet interfaces.

The Singles Phenomenon

This preference for human contact particularly affects single people, who increasingly value genuine human conversation. Tesco, the British supermarket chain, has begun removing automated checkout points and reinstating human cashiers after discovering that many single people's only daily human contact occurs during grocery shopping. When this represents your sole human interaction, it becomes tremendously valuable, and customers will pay premium prices for it.

This creates competing forces: we can automate learning and teaching whilst removing human factors, but simultaneously, people increasingly crave human contact and will pay higher prices for it. It will be fascinating to observe which direction various industries ultimately choose.

Realistic Expectations

AI provides useful feedback and encouragement when properly implemented and properly controlled, offering genuine opportunities whilst remaining limited to capabilities that humans can also provide. This is why I encourage caution and careful consideration rather than adopting technology simply because it exists.

The setup process requires enormous resources, and you can often provide substantial human interaction for the cost of implementing customised AI systems for students. Some claim AI enhances inclusion and educational access, but this isn't accurate. I dispute claims about enhanced inclusion because these systems extend screen time for individual students rather than promoting collaboration with other people. This represents exclusion, not inclusion, just like social media, which should be renamed to antisocial media.

Conclusion: The Path Forward

As we've examined throughout this chapter, artificial intelligence in education presents a complex landscape of genuine benefits alongside significant limitations and concerns. Whilst AI can support certain aspects of learning - particularly in making education more accessible and providing specific types of personalised feedback - it cannot and should not replace the fundamental human elements that make education meaningful.

The critical question isn't whether AI can contribute to education (it can, in specific circumstances), but whether We are willing to accept the social costs and limitations that accompany its implementation. As educators and learners, we must maintain our humanity at the centre of educational experiences, using AI as a carefully selected tool rather than allowing it to become the focus of our educational environments.

The future of education lies not in choosing between human and artificial intelligence, but in thoughtfully determining when and how AI tools can genuinely enhance human teaching and learning whilst preserving the irreplaceable elements of human connection, creativity, and wisdom that define meaningful education.

6: The Myth of the Machine Teacher – Why Educators Remain Irreplaceable

Artificial Intelligence (AI) is heralded by some as a revolution in education. The word “revolution” is thrown around so freely that it risks losing any real meaning. Only future generations can judge if what you were doing was revolutionising.

Here is the definition of revolution from Oxford Learners Dictionary:

revolution *noun*

B2

/ˌrevəˈluːʃn/

/ˌrevəˈluːʃn/

1 ★ B2 [countable, uncountable] an attempt, by a large number of people, to change the government of a country, especially by violent action

- *a **socialist revolution***
- *the outbreak of the French Revolution in 1789*
- *The shooting and killing of thirty people started a revolution.*
- *The country appears to be on the brink of revolution.*

With that in mid, how many of the new technologies are revolutionary? Answer: NONE. It is used just as a marketing term by desperate sales people.

I refuse to adopt that term for one simple reason: I do not see AI as a revolution and neither does it fit into the definition of a revolution. At best, it is a tool - one that must remain firmly in the hands of teachers and professors, with human educators at the centre of learning.

The glossy presentations from technology companies will have us believe that AI will replace vast numbers of teaching roles, automating everything from marking to lesson planning, freeing educators for more "important" work, which is totally nonsense if you listen to what this "important" work is. "Learning coaches" they call it.

People who shall act as extended sales people for the tech industry. It is an alluring sales pitch - but it is also deeply misleading. The reality, as I have observed and as [Apple's own 2025 research report] confirms, is that generative AI cannot reason, cannot truly think, and cannot make value-based judgements. Strip away the clever prompting and pattern-matching, and these systems collapse under the weight of tasks requiring multi-step reasoning or abstract logic. They guess - often based on statistical likelihoods, not genuine understanding.

And yet, despite these limitations, there is an aggressive push to insert AI into classrooms and lecture halls. Governments are lobbied, universities courted, and schools promised "efficiency" gains that rarely materialise once the full set-up, oversight, and correction time is factored in. And when the investments have been made, it is too expensive getting out again. It is a traditional IT-sales strategy.

More worryingly, the marketing narrative rarely addresses the most fundamental truth: teaching is more than information delivery. It is about trust, relationships, empathy, ethics, and human connection - elements which no algorithm can replicate. AI cannot teach to decency, compassion, solidarity or many other crucial human characteristics.

In the pre-AI classroom, the teacher is the focal point: knowledge-holder, motivator, and moral compass. AI, if left unchecked, risks shifting that centre of gravity away from the human educator and towards a faceless, centralised system. This is not progress; it is a dangerous erosion of what makes education truly transformative. The so-called "evolution" of the teacher into a mere "facilitator" of AI-generated content is not an upgrade - it is a downgrading of the profession and a narrowing of the student experience.

Even the much-touted "efficiencies" of AI must be treated with great suspicion. Automated grading of quizzes has existed for decades, long before the current AI hype took off. Handling timetables and basic communications? These functions were automated years ago. The claim that AI will replace creative and technical jobs is, as Apple's findings confirm, technologically unfounded. The machines do not and will not possess creativity or genuine problem-solving ability.

The emotional intelligence of a human educator - detecting fear or passion in a student before it is spoken, sensing exclusion in group work, adapting tone and approach to preserve dignity and motivation - cannot be replicated by data-driven systems. And yet, we are told to trust these systems with monitoring "engagement" and "progress," as if such qualities can be reduced to a dashboard metric.

The truth is this: No matter how much money is poured into AI marketing, the human educator remains irreplaceable. Teachers inspire, they comfort, they challenge, they connect and they guide the students so that they can navigate complex societies with both passion and scepticisms and always critically evaluate what is presented.

They are becoming education leaders not because they can outpace an algorithm in recalling facts, but because they bring wisdom, humour, cultural understanding, and emotional depth to the learning process.

If there is to be a role for AI in education, it must be as a servant, not a master. Educators - not IT-corporations - must decide how, when, and whether to use it. The strategic direction of schools and universities must remain in the hands of those who understand that learning is a human act. Without this safeguard, we risk a cold, mechanical classroom where students are managed and manipulated by machines, rather than mentored by people.

7: The Myths, Risks, and Realities of AI in Education

The public narrative around artificial intelligence in education has been dominated by grand promises, sleek marketing, and breathless headlines about an impending "AI revolution" in the classroom. But beneath this glitter lies a far more complex - and in many cases, troubling - reality. AI's limitations are numerous, its ethical foundations shaky, and its supposed ability to "replace" educators is, in practice, an illusion.

For years now, I have cautioned educators to resist the relentless pressure from technology vendors, political leaders, and even institutional management, who often advocate AI adoption without truly understanding the technology or its potential fatal consequences. The result is a widespread push to force AI into areas of education where it is, quite simply, inadequate.

The Illusion of Replacement

Let's address one of the most persistent fears first: the idea that AI will take over the teaching profession. Yes, some, who usually don't know what they are talking about, may claim that AI can replace human educators, but this belief stems largely from a lack of understanding about what teaching actually entails. Education is not just about delivering information - it is about human connection, context, and moral judgment.

The reality? Any school bold enough to replace human teachers with AI robots will surely regret it quickly and reinstate the very people they dismissed - probably at higher salaries due to increased bargaining power. AI cannot replicate empathy, interpret complex contexts, or make morally sound decisions. These are distinctly human capabilities.

Here is an example:

"Ed," the AI Chatbot in Los Angeles Unified School District (LAUSD)

What happened: In March 2024, LAUSD launched "Ed," an AI-powered chatbot designed to assist with tasks like tracking grades, attendance, and generating individualised learning plans—acting as a student assistant.

Outcome: The project collapsed in June 2024 after the company behind it, AllHere Education, went under. LAUSD shut down the AI chatbot entirely.

Result: This failure underscored the importance of human oversight and control in education systems. While human teachers may not have been explicitly rehired in that instant, the shutdown itself was a de facto reinstatement of human-led processes in classrooms.

Risks in Implementation and Administration

One of the most under-appreciated risks is not technological at all - it is organisational. AI systems are expensive to implement, require substantial administrative overhead, and often fail to deliver value unless deployed at significant scale. For smaller institutions, the cost–benefit ratio is almost always unfavourable, and the promised "efficiency gains" evaporate under real-world scrutiny, lack of skills and poor strategic and operational fit.

Even when the system is technically functional, AI's recommendations can be dangerously inappropriate. In a simulation exercise I used at a business school recently, an AI-driven pandemic model suggested that killing 20,000 people in a single city would be an acceptable trade-off to prevent disease spread to millions. Logically consistent? Perhaps. Morally disgusting? Absolutely.

Bias: The Silent Saboteur

Every AI system inherits the biases of its training data and when it is using synthetic data, these biases become even more dominant because existing patterns become amplified and not diversified. Whether it is racially skewed grading, language-based discrimination, or cultural prejudice, these biases are not theoretical - they are [well documented].

Example:

Consider AI-assisted job interviews: candidates are graded on their facial expressions, speed of speech, and language fluency. Those whose first language is not English are automatically disadvantaged, regardless of actual competence. Such biases don't merely "risk" disadvantaging people - they actively do so.

In education, the consequences can be severe: biased grading systems, flawed performance predictions, and exclusionary recommendations. A student's future could be derailed not by poor academic ability but by the blind prejudices encoded into an algorithm.

Most of the AI systems I have surveyed are highly intransparent. That means that you as a leather or professor won't be able to fully explain to a student why he or she has received a certain grade or being given a certain recommendation. How will you feel in such a situation? Will you defend the student or the system?

Privacy Under Siege

AI's hunger for data is insatiable. Whether grading, recommending resources, or tracking engagement, these systems often require the aggregation of vast amounts of personal information - not just academic records, but sometimes health data, behavioural patterns, and even location tracking.

The dangers here are manifold: data breaches, unethical profiling, and long-term misuse of stored information. Students must have the right to know exactly what is collected, how it is used, and - critically - the right to opt out without penalty. This is not just good practice; it is a moral imperative.

Here are some recent examples of data breaches in the education industry. And the more data we collect the more valuable they become to hackers and other criminals

Massive Cyberattacks in India (2023–24)

A report based on the CyberPeace Foundation's "e-Kawach" initiative found that Indian educational institutions endured **over 200,000 cyberattacks** and **nearly 400,000 data breaches** within nine months. These incidents included phishing, deepfake misuse, and exam paper leaks.

Diksha App Data Exposure (2022)

India's widely used educational platform **Diksha** inadvertently exposed data from **over 1 million teachers** and **600,000 students** due to an unsecured cloud server, accessible since at least 2018.

NYU Admissions Data Leak (March 2025)

Hackers defaced New York University's website and leaked admissions data for **over 3 million applicants**, including test scores, financial aid information, majors, zip codes, and background data.

Bangalore University Record Tampering (June 2025)

A breach within Karnataka's UUCMS platform led to the unauthorized alteration of academic marks for 55 BCA students, highlighting weaknesses in centralised educational systems.

Pennsylvania State Education Association (PSEA) Breach

In July 2024, a ransomware attack breached PSEA's database, compromising personal information—like Social Security numbers, financial, and health data—of **over 500,000 educators and associated individuals**.

Therefore. You should bepare for the best data security, which is expensive and you should prepare for when it is you who has to explain why sensible data about your students have been stolen or made public.

Are you ready for that?

The Over-Reliance Trap

Over-reliance on AI in education fosters passivity among students and laziness among educators. I have seen students submit AI-generated presentations with no comprehension of the content, thinking they could shortcut their way to a grade. It fails them academically and intellectually.

Teachers, too, risk delegating too much to AI - grading, content selection, even the creation of teaching materials. This erosion of professional engagement ultimately undermines trust, authenticity, and creativity.

Technology, when left unchecked, has a habit of producing uniformity and mediocrity. Just as modern car design has converged into dull sameness under the influence of CAD optimisation, education will become soulless and irrelevant-when shaped primarily by algorithms.

The Digital Divide

AI adoption is not evenly distributed. Wealthier institutions can afford sophisticated systems; poorer ones cannot. The result is an educational "A team" and "B team", deepening existing inequalities. And within the same society, those who are digitally adept thrive, while those without the skills - or access - are left behind.

Wealthier institutions and schools will also use AI more critically and keep the IT vendors on short leach while less prosperous institutions might be tempted to let the big-tech companies unchecked and give them free hand to steal all the information they can get hold of in return for access to mediocre systems.

I am however absolutely not certain that those falling for big-techs sales tricks will be the long-term winners. I hope and think that it will become a brand value that courses are NOT AI developed or taught.

What do you think?

Education is Relational, Not Merely Informational

At its core, education is built on relationships - between teacher/professor and student, between peers, and between the learner and the real world in all its beautiful diversity.

No AI system can replicate the subtlety of trust, care, and human connection. The reassuring touch on a shoulder, the unspoken recognition of a struggling pupil's distress - these are things no machine can mimic.

The Need for Ethical Guardrails

Institutions must establish - and enforce - clear policies on AI use, ensuring transparency, accountability, and the ability to erase personal data upon request. Vendor-driven decision-making should be avoided at all costs; commercial interests rarely align perfectly with educational values.

In one of the final chapters of this book I will share my recommendation on how you develop the right policies and explain more in depth why they have to be developed and discussed before you choose any technology at all.

In summary:

AI in education is not a neutral tool; it carries inherent risks - ethical, technical, social, and cultural. It can misinterpret, exclude, and dehumanise. Without critical oversight, it could erode the very qualities that make education meaningful.

The responsibility lies with educators, not vendors, to determine where AI belongs - and, more importantly, where it does not.

8: The Mirage of Fairness: Bias, Inequality and the Illusion of Objectivity in AI

Whenever technology companies talk about artificial intelligence in education, the conversation inevitably drifts towards promises of fairness, objectivity and neutrality. The narrative is seductive: machines, unlike humans, will assess without bias; algorithms will treat everyone equally; data will replace subjective judgement.

It sounds marvellous - until you look closely.

The reality is that AI systems are not born in a vacuum. They are created by human beings, trained on human data, and steeped in human decisions - and that means they inherit our prejudices. In many cases, they don't just replicate bias; they amplify it.

I have seen it time and again. The data fed into these systems already carries the fingerprints of existing inequality. If a system is trained on historical exam results, it will reproduce the patterns of advantage and disadvantage baked into those results. If past hiring practices have excluded certain groups, the AI will faithfully recommend more of the same.

One of my greatest frustrations is the smug assurance from tech vendors that their products are "bias-free" because they have "removed demographic variables" such as gender or ethnicity. This is naïve at best and disingenuous at worst. You can strip out the obvious identifiers, but the bias remains embedded in the patterns - postcode, school history, even hobbies can act as proxies for socio-economic status or ethnicity. The system will still "learn" the inequality.

And yet, these AI tools are being pushed into our schools and universities under the banner of fairness. The danger is obvious: when bias is hidden inside a machine, it becomes harder to challenge. A teacher's prejudice, however unpleasant, can be called out. But an algorithm's judgement? How will you do that?

That comes wrapped in a coating of mathematical inevitability. People are far less likely to question it - and far more likely to accept it as fact. That is also why you see a lot of people on LinkedIn bragging about that they are data-driven. By that statement they try to lure people into believing that they are more trustworthy, which of course is pure nonsense.

I often use the example of student progress tracking. On the surface, it seems like a good idea: AI can monitor performance, flag at-risk students, and recommend interventions. But what exactly is it measuring? If the system is tuned to reward students who hand in work on time, it will penalise those dealing with difficult personal circumstances - illness, caring responsibilities, mental health struggles. These complexities are invisible to the algorithm.

A teacher or professor, on the other hand, can spot when a student is under strain for reasons unrelated to academic ability. They can choose compassion over cold scoring. An

AI system cannot. And that is precisely one of the main reasons why I worry about the creeping normalisation of automated judgement in education.

The sales pitch for AI is often dressed up in grand social ambitions like: widening participation, closing attainment gaps, levelling the playing field. I wish I could believe it. But when you study how these systems actually work, you see a very different story. The rich still get richer - because they already fit the system's definition of "success". Those outside the norm are quietly filtered out.

This is why I keep coming back to the same point in my talks and lectures: AI in education must never be accepted uncritically. We must question not just the outputs but also the inputs; not just the results but the values embedded in the code. You can learn more about my speeches and workshops on AI in education at:

https://majlergaard.com/AI

Because if we allow ourselves to believe the myth of machine objectivity, we risk entrenching the very inequalities we claim to be solving - all the while congratulating ourselves on our "progress". Once the damage has happened to the students, the education institutions and the society there is no way you can undo it, just like you can't squeeze the toothpaste back into the tube.

9: Black Boxes and Fragile Promises: Transparency, Accountability and the Ethics Void

If bias is the silent poison in AI, then opacity is the perfect hiding place.

One of the most troubling aspects of AI in education is how little we – the education professionals - are allowed to see of what's actually going on inside the machine. These systems are often described as black boxes - we can observe what goes in and what comes out, but the inner workings remain hidden. And in many cases, that secrecy isn't accidental; it is by design. And that is a severely damaging factor for the deployment of AI in education.

That is because trust in the relationship between the professor and the student is paramount. And that trust can only be maintained if there is traceability, transparency and accountability in every type of communication. AI systems cannot and will not provide that. A student must have the option of being explained why he or she got the grade they did, or why the professor recommended a certain reading at a particular point in time.

And the teachers and professors are accountable for the grades they give and the quality of the teaching they provide. Students can complain and an investigative process is initiated. How will you ever do that with an AI machine that acts as a black box? You can't which is why the fundamental element of mutual trust is destroyed when using AI in education.

The technology vendors manipulation

Technology vendors call it "protecting intellectual property." I call it "dodging accountability." If we cannot examine the rules and data that underpin an AI machines decision, then we cannot meaningfully challenge its errors - and that is a dangerous precedent to set in education.

I have spoken with teachers and professors who have been handed AI-generated reports on their students without any explanation of how the system arrived at its conclusions. "The model says the student is underperforming," they're told. When they ask why, the response is a shrug or, worse, "It is too complicated to explain." That's not good enough! We would never accept a human assessor refusing to justify a grade; so why should we accept it from a machine?

The problem runs deeper when we remember that universities and schools are under increasing pressure to "optimise" resources and standardise performance. AI fits neatly into that managerial data-driven mindset - but it strips away the humanity. A dashboard metric becomes the final word on a student's ability, regardless of context, nuance, or circumstance.

Then there's the question of responsibility. When an AI machine makes a wrong call - which it will - who is to blame? The teacher who used it? The program manager who approved it? The vendor who built it? Or the policy-makers who pushed for its adoption? The uncomfortable truth is that responsibility tends to dissolve in a fog of finger-pointing.

I have seen this before in other industries: when no single person or legal entity owns the decision, accountability evaporates. In education, that's catastrophic. The stakes are too high to allow a decision that affects a student's future to be made by a system that no one can, or will, take responsibility for.

Of course, technology companies know that "ethics" sells. Many now have glossy AI ethics charters and principles proudly displayed on their websites. But dig beneath the surface, and you find that most of these guidelines are voluntary, unenforceable, and riddled with vague platitudes like "we strive to be fair" and "we value transparency" - without any clear mechanism for proving it or anr clear definition of the responsibility that they have. That is why you have to define and describe the responsibilities the IT vendors have to live up to, and also the sanctions that will be imposed if they fail to live up to their obligations.

What is true transparency?

True transparency isn't just about publishing a PDF with nice-sounding words. It means opening the code, revealing the data sources, and allowing independent scrutiny. It means admitting when your system gets it wrong and explaining why. Until that becomes standard practice, these so-called "ethical commitments" are no more than marketing exercises.

And let me be clear: AI is not a neutral force that simply "exists" in education. It is a set of deliberate choices made by humans - what to measure, what to prioritise, what to ignore. Each of those choices carries value judgements, and those values will shape how students are taught, assessed, and supported.

Which is why, whenever I am asked whether I "trust" AI in education, my answer is the same:

I trust the teacher or professor, not the tool.

I trust the judgement of someone who knows the student's name, background, and struggles - not a black box model optimised for efficiency targets.

If AI machines have a role to play, it should be as an assistant under human oversight, not an unchallengeable authority. Because once we hand over our decision-making to systems we cannot see, cannot question, and cannot hold to account, we haven't just automated education - we've surrendered it to the most greedy people and organisations on this planet.

10: The Price of Data: AI, Student Privacy, and the Ethics We Cannot Ignore

Artificial intelligence has arrived in education dressed in the language of progress: efficiency, personalisation, innovation. Yet beneath the glossy surface lies an uncomfortable truth - one we cannot afford to ignore. The very systems claiming to support our learners are often harvesting their most intimate data, building detailed profiles, and using those profiles for purposes that extend far beyond education.

It is here, at the intersection of technology, ethics, and human dignity, that my critique begins.

Data Is the Currency – and Students Are the Product

We are told - soothingly - that AI tools collect data to "personalise learning" and "support student progress." But anyone who has paid attention to the commercial history of data knows this is only part of the story. The reality is more troubling.

AI systems in education do not simply note a student's quiz score or time spent on an assignment. They can monitor location, device type, browsing behaviour, even the time of day a learner logs on. The more sophisticated the system, the deeper and broader its data reach. And the more opaque the process, the greater the risk to student safety and privacy.

In truth, the education sector is simply replaying the same pattern we have seen with Google Maps, social media, and online booking systems - where the service is free or low-cost not because companies are feeling charitable, but because the user *is* the product. Your behaviour, preferences, and identity are what's being sold to organisations who can profit from it in various ways.

And in totalitarian regimes like China, Russia, North Korea and soon the USA, the governments will collect data to control, manipulate and punish people.

The Surveillance Problem

In an age where surveillance cameras and online tracking have normalised constant observation, we risk dragging that culture into classrooms and lecture halls. AI-powered monitoring tools - whether for attendance, performance, or "safety" - inevitably alter behaviour. Students who know they are watched may self-censor, take fewer creative risks, or withdraw socially. We have seen that in for instance China. Here are some examples:

University Classrooms (Political Sensitivity)

Studies have shown that Chinese students often avoid raising politically sensitive questions in class discussions because of the **presence of classroom surveillance cameras** and the risk of being reported.

A 2021 article in *The China Quarterly* described how surveillance infrastructure on campuses contributes to a "culture of caution," where students refrain from openly criticizing government policies.

Online Learning During COVID-19

When Chinese universities moved to online platforms (like Tencent Classroom, DingTalk, or Zoom), many students reported **withdrawing from debates or avoiding critical comments** on politics, society, or history.

The reason: they knew the platforms were monitored, and they feared recordings could be stored and reviewed later.

Student Monitoring Apps

Some Chinese universities required students to install "student behaviour apps" on their phones to track study and attendance.

Interviews with students (documented in ethnographic studies) revealed that they **self-censored social media posts and group chat discussions** to avoid attracting attention from authorities.

International Classrooms with Chinese Students

Chinese students studying abroad have also been documented as **self-censoring in foreign classrooms** (e.g., about Hong Kong, Xinjiang, or Taiwan), fearing surveillance by classmates or potential repercussions for their families back home. This has been noted in reports by *Human Rights Watch (2021)* and in academic work by scholars like Clive Hamilton.

So it is important to remember and be aware of, that the more information you let systems collect about you and your students the higher risk there is will be used to control and manipulation.

I grew up in a world where a day of unsupervised exploration was unremarkable. Today's young people, by contrast, face a reality where their movements, clicks, and keystrokes can be traced at any moment. In education, such conditions do not foster curiosity - they breed anxiety.

When parents can track their children's movements all day long from their mobile phones, that generates anxiety from an early age.

The danger is not simply overreach, but the subtle erosion of trust between learner and institution or child and parent. When surveillance is hidden, or when students later discover its extent, the betrayal is profound. And once the trust is lost, it is rarely regained. Educational institutions must ask themselves if they are willing to take that risk and why would they want to do it?

The Illusion of Consent

Many institutions assure parents and students that "consent" has been obtained. Yet too often, consent is a box ticked under pressure or without genuine understanding of what is at stake. Transparency is not a courtesy - it is a duty. Students and families must know *what* is collected, *why*, *for how long* it is kept, and *who* has access.

If your institution cannot obtain that information from a technology vendor, the conclusion is clear: do not use the system. Lack of transparency is not a minor inconvenience; it is a red flag.

Beyond the Minimum Standards

Regulations such as the EU's General Data Protection Regulation (GDPR) have raised the floor for data protection. But meeting the minimum legal standard is not enough. Schools and universities must actively *exceed* those requirements, guided by strong ethical principles that put students welfare and safety far ahead of convenience or cost-saving.

Practical measures are not glamorous, but they are essential: choose tools with strong encryption, limit access to sensitive records, audit data collection regularly, and - crucially - ask whether a piece of data truly needs to be collected at all. In most cases, the honest answer will be "no."

The Bias Built Into the Machine

AI systems inherit and amplify biases as I have mentioned earlier - whether in grading, recommendations, or behavioural predictions. Combine academic data with information from a student's smartwatch, social media activity, or geolocation, and you create the potential for deeply unethical correlations. Imagine a system suggesting a student's poor maths performance might be solved by weight loss - an intrusion not only absurd but potentially harmful.

Such examples may sound extreme, yet they are the logical outcome of unrestrained data integration. The more data points you feed an algorithm, the more confident it becomes in making pronouncements it has no business making.

The Educator's Responsibility

Teachers and professors are not passive bystanders in this debate, and that is one of the reason I have written this book. They/we are the first line of defence - mentors not only in subject knowledge, but in digital ethics. This means equipping students to understand and protect their own data, and ensuring no one feels coerced into surrendering personal information for fear of academic disadvantage.

If admiration for technology blinds us to these responsibilities, we have already failed.

Questions We Must Ask Ourselves

Before embracing any AI tool in education, we must confront difficult questions like:

- What data are we collecting now, and why?
- How is it stored, shared, and protected?
- Are students and, where relevant, parents fully informed - and do they truly have a choice?
- Can we guarantee that our technology vendors are acting lawfully, ethically, and transparently?

Your answers will determine not only the safety of your students, but the integrity of our profession.

Closing Thoughts

Data is powerful, valuable, and - if mishandled - dangerous. In education, where trust is the foundation of learning, any breach of that trust is unacceptable. My position is not anti-technology; it is pro-student and pro-professor. If an AI system cannot meet the highest standards of transparency, security, and ethics, it has no place in our classrooms or virtual learning spaces.

Innovation without integrity is not progress - it is surrender as stated earlier.

Fortunately we have a nightmare to look at: China. Let us not go there

11: Challenging Tradition: Why AI Is Just a Tool

Whenever new technology emerges, there's a predictable chorus: "This will revolutionise everything!" We have heard it with the internet, smartphones, blockchain, Internet of Things (IoT), interactive whiteboards - and now artificial intelligence. The education sector is currently being told, with evangelical fervour, that AI will "replace outdated systems" and "transform learning forever."

Let me repeat myself: AI is not a revolution. Please see the definition of revolution in one of the earlier chapters. It is a tool - nothing more, nothing less. And in education, it will never replace teachers, professors, or the human connections that make learning truly effective.

Yet the people selling these systems often paint a completely different picture. They will have us believe that before AI, education was stuck in the Stone Age, with dusty textbooks and rigid routines, and that salvation has now arrived in the form of their software. That is pure, primitive marketing spin, not reality.

Why Traditions Exist in the First Place

Many education systems were designed during the industrial era, around 1900, with fixed timetables, standardised tests, and a focus on uniform skills. This approach wasn't dreamt up by accident - it matched the needs of the time, preparing workers and farmers for industrial roles.

Since then, education has evolved continuously without AI's help. Age-based progression has already loosened; students of all ages drop in and out of education throughout their lives. I supervise PhD candidates in their fifties and sixties who bring decades of practical experience to their academic work. That flexibility was achieved without machine learning algorithms.

Likewise, teaching has moved far beyond the old "sage on the stage" model. We now have project-based, activity-led, and collaborative learning approaches that long pre-date the current AI hype. Change has happened because educators saw value in it - not because a tech company saw a new profit model and then invented a fake need.

It has actually become a tragic-comic norm, that tech companies invent a technology and then try to invent a need for it afterwards. It is often pathetic to watch especially for someone like me who have spend so many years in large, global tech companies and know their approach inside-out. AI follow that model, and the more money that is put into AI companies (where none of them are profitable) the more extreme the marketing campaigns become.

You should also think about that all these AI systems for the education industry are based on technologies from companies that all loses truckloads of money every day. What do you think will happen to your investment when the bubble burst?

Personalisation – and Its Price

One of AI's big selling points in education is "personalised learning." In theory, this means adapting the pace and content to each learner's needs. In practice, it means feeding vast quantities of student data into systems you do not fully control, often built by companies with opaque practices and short-term commercial motives.

Yes, personalisation can be beneficial - but only if we retain transparency, accountability, and strict data protection. Buy a "black box" solution, and you forfeit that control. The supposed benefits then come at a very high cost: loss of privacy, reduced trust, increased surveillance and a reliance on a system that cannot respond with cultural or emotional intelligence.

And let's remember: personalisation itself is not new. Teachers have been differentiating their approach for decades - without spying on students or sending their data to third parties.

The Self-Centred Learning Trap

AI advocates love to present a "paradigm shift" from standardised learning to hyper-individualised paths. On paper it sounds exciting - student-centred learning, self-reflection, self-awareness, self-direction. But look closely, and you see what's missing: collaboration, mutual understanding, and learning from each other. The self prefix on everything leads to egocentric, lonely students with even more limited social competences than what we see today. Social media killed the fun part of living and made people more lonely than ever before in history.

It is an egocentric model: *me, me, me* - a learner isolated in front of a machine, externally managed and surveilled, with little room for co-creation or group achievement.

I find that vision and development deeply troubling. Societies don't thrive on atomised individuals loyal to systems rather than each other. And yet AI-generated images of "classrooms of the future" almost always show solitary students, eyes locked on screens, not talking to a soul. Is that what we want?

I know I don't. I only know I will fight against it with all my power.

Flexible Learning – Lessons from COVID

Some praise AI's ability to enable flexible, "anytime, anywhere" learning. But we learned during the COVID pandemic that while remote study can deliver content, it often damages the social and emotional dimensions of education – the personal, emotional motivation.

We saw students become stressed, depressed, and bored. They might have acquired certain factual skills, but they missed out on the group work, cultural exchange, and spontaneous interactions that underpin real learning. You can't develop empathy, teamwork, or resilience by staring at a screen in isolation.

The Myth of the "AI Age"

I reject the notion that we live in an "Age of AI." We live in an age where AI exists, much like pens, projectors, or word processors exist. It is a tool - sometimes useful, sometimes not. It doesn't deserve to "drive" education and you shouldn't let it. Human beings - education professionals - must drive education, using AI only where it genuinely adds value without undermining our core human values.

And let's not kid ourselves: much of the resistance from educators to AI is not a technophobe fear, but sound judgement. In my 25 years of teaching at business schools and universities worldwide, I have seen countless examples of change embraced - when it benefits students. Resistance often means the technology is unsuitable, unproven, or irrelevant to the real needs of learners.

Sales Pitches vs. Reality

AI vendors often accuse educators of being behind the times. That comes from sales people, who know nothing about education. They have no understanding of how teaching works, how much it has evolved, or how strong the emotional bonds are between students and educators. They underestimate the centrality of trust, empathy, and shared human experience in learning. They only have their focus on the next commission-based paycheck.

A telling example: during COVID, Zoom's own executives demanded that the staff returned to physical offices because creativity and collaboration suffered in remote work. If even the video conferencing giant recognises the limits of screen-based interaction, shouldn't we learn from that lesson in education?

Creativity Is Not Innovation

One final thought: true innovation has purpose and direction. Creativity without purpose might be fun and entertaining, but in education we must ask whether a change actually improves learning outcomes. Implementing AI simply because it is "new" is not innovation - it is distraction.

Before adopting any AI system, we must ask:

- Does it align with our educational values?
- Does it enhance well-being, inclusion, and lifelong learning - or undermine them?
- Does it foster human connection - or erode it?

Because if the answer to that last question is "erode," we should walk away.

12: The Great AI Deception - Why Education Isn't Broken

When I first encountered the wave of artificial intelligence evangelists descending upon educational institutions, I was reminded of something I had witnessed countless times during my twenty years in the technology industry: the classic sales pitch that begins with declaring the customer's current situation utterly antiquated. "Your education system is stuck in the Stone Age," they proclaim with evangelical fervour, "but fear not - AI shall deliver you into the promised land of personalised learning!"

What struck me most profoundly was not the boldness of these claims, but rather how fundamentally they misrepresented the reality of modern education. Having spent the better part of my career both in technology development and later as a business school professor and business owner, I have witnessed this pattern repeatedly: Technology companies creating problems that don't exist in order to sell solutions nobody particularly needs. With them, they drag people who go from one commercial failure to the next always claining – THIS is going to be revolutionising.

The Myth of Educational Stagnation

The narrative being peddled by AI vendors is breathtakingly simplistic: traditional education systems, they claim, were designed for the industrial age, with their rigid timetables, standardised tests, and one-size-fits-all approaches. They paint a picture of teachers as mere "information providers" standing rigidly before passive students, mechanically delivering content from dusty textbooks.

This characterisation would be laughable were it not so widely accepted without question. During my years teaching at business schools and universities across the world, I have witnessed a continuous evolution in educational practice that began decades before ChatGPT uttered its first hallucination. We have moved from teacher-centred to student-centred approaches, embraced project-based learning, developed sophisticated assessment methods that go far beyond rote memorisation, and created flexible pathways that accommodate diverse learning styles and life circumstances.

I often tell my students - many of whom are professionals in their fifties and sixties pursuing advanced degrees - that the very fact they're sitting in my classroom demonstrates how utterly wrong the "age-based progression" narrative is. Education has already adapted to become a lifelong endeavour, with people dropping in and out of formal learning throughout their careers.

The Tool Trap

Here's the fundamental truth that AI evangelists desperately want you to forget: artificial intelligence is a tool. Not a revolution, not a paradigm shift, not the centre of a new educational universe - simply a tool, much like a hammer or a calculator. Yet listen to the marketing materials, attend the conferences, read the breathless predictions, and You will encounter language that positions AI as the protagonist in education's story, with human educators relegated to supporting roles. It is almost like a new-age religious movement.

This linguistic sleight of hand isn't accidental. By framing AI as a "partner" or positioning us in an "age of AI," technology companies are attempting to fundamentally restructure the power dynamics within education. They want you to believe that resistance to their products stems from fear of change or technological incompetence, when in reality it often stems from a clear-eyed assessment of what these systems can and cannot do and a clear awareness of the power the big tech try to get over the education sector.

I have seen this pattern before. During my years in the technology sector, we were remarkably sophisticated at manipulating potential clients, making them feel antiquated for not embracing whatever solution we happened to be selling. The playbook hasn't changed: create anxiety about falling behind, present your product as inevitable, then position any scepticism as backwards-thinking resistance to progress. It works!

What AI Cannot Do

The most glaring omission in AI-in-education discourse is honest discussion of fundamental limitations. And you can't have, and should not have these discussions with the tech companies that provide these systems. They will never give you an honest answer as their only objective is to increase sales. These systems cannot form emotional connections with learners. They cannot understand cultural or emotional contexts in meaningful ways. They cannot demonstrate genuine empathy or provide the kind of nuanced feedback that comes from years of the educational experience you have. They cannot inspire, motivate on a human level, or adapt to the countless variables that influence learning in real-time.

Most critically, they cannot replace the social and collaborative aspects of learning that we discovered were so vital during the COVID pandemic. When educational institutions worldwide were forced into remote learning, we didn't celebrate the arrival of personalised, AI-driven education. Instead, we witnessed increased depression, anxiety, and isolation amongst students. We learned that the "flexible, any-time, anywhere" model that AI proponents champion can be profoundly damaging to human wellbeing, especially combined with constant assessment and constant feedback on fixed performance metrics.

Even Zoom - one of the primary beneficiaries of remote interaction - recognised this reality when they mandated that their employees return to physical offices because creativity and innovation had suffered during remote work. If a company built around virtual interaction acknowledges the irreplaceable value of human presence, shouldn't educators be even more sceptical of claims that AI can substitute for human connection?

The Social Cost of Individualisation

Perhaps the most troubling aspect of AI-driven educational vision is its relentless focus on individualisation. Every promise centres on the individual learner: personalised paths, customised content, individual pacing, self-directed learning. The language is telling - it is all "self" and "me" with precious little about "us", "we" or "together." Is it really the values you want to promote to your students and in the society?

This represents a fundamentally impoverished view of what education should accomplish. Yes, we want to meet individual learning needs, but education's broader purpose includes teaching people to work collaboratively, to learn from diverse perspectives, to negotiate differences, to contribute to group efforts. These distinctly human skills cannot be developed through individualised interaction with AI systems.

I find it genuinely frightening that we might produce graduates who are highly personalised in their learning but utterly unprepared for the collaborative, messy, emotionally complex reality of human society. When I observe AI-generated imagery depicting educational futures, I invariably see isolated individuals staring at screens, cut off from human interaction. Is this really the educational vision we want to pursue, where all interaction between humans has been hijacked by technology? We have seen that with social media, that are anything but social. People are sitting alone in front of of their screens or mobile phones, feeling miserably lonely despite being connected to millions.

A psychologist once told me that the reason why are so hooked on music from the 60'ies, 70'ies and 80'ies is that it reminds of of a time that has gone. A time were we were together with real people, flirted in real life, and we didn't have these bloody mobile phones glued to our hands. We had our eyes and ears open to the world - not the curated, commercial version presented on the screen.

As an educator, you have a choice! Use your voice and your influence.

The Resistance Narrative

Technology companies have a ready explanation for any hesitation about adopting their commercial solutions:

Resistance to change.

They characterise educators as conservative, backwards-looking, afraid of losing power to technological innovation. This narrative serves their interests by positioning scepticism as an emotional failing rather than a rational response to questionable value propositions.

In my consulting work helping organisations navigate cultural change, I have learned that resistance often signals wisdom rather than obstinacy. People resist changes that don't clearly benefit them or their work. When experienced educators express scepticism about AI systems, we should listen to their concerns rather than dismissing them as technophobia. And they resist because they care. If they didn't care, they would just walk away. So when people resist – we better listen and learn.

The resistance narrative also ignores the reality that educational institutions have continuously adopted beneficial technologies. Interactive whiteboards, multimedia presentations, online resources, digital assessment tools - educators have embraced technologies that genuinely enhance their work. The difference is that these tools remained tools, supporting rather than supplanting human judgement and connection.

A More Honest Assessment

None of this is to suggest that AI has no place in education. Like any tool, it may prove useful in specific contexts for particular purposes. The question isn't whether AI can contribute anything to education - it is whether the contribution justifies the costs, risks, and the fundamental changes being proposed.

What frustrates me most about current discourse is the absence of nuanced evaluation. We are presented with a false choice: embrace AI transformation or remain mired in educational prehistory. This binary thinking serves the tech vendors' interests but poorly serves students, educators, and society.

A responsible approach would acknowledge that:

- Education has been evolving continuously, with or without AI.
- Human connection remains central to effective learning
- Individualisation isn't inherently superior to collaborative learning.
- Tools must serve educational purposes rather than drive them.
- Scepticism usually indicate wisdom rather than fear.

As we move forward, I encourage you to maintain what I call "open scepticism" - remaining curious about potential benefits whilst insisting on evidence, transparency, and alignment with educational values that have served us well so far. The future of education doesn't require choosing between human wisdom and artificial intelligence; it requires keeping AI in its proper place as a tool in service of fundamentally human educational purposes.

In the following chapters, I will explore what responsible AI integration might look like, examine the real risks that accompany these systems, and consider how educators can maintain agency in an environment where powerful technological and political interests are working to diminish it.

13: The Faustian Bargain - Privacy, Data, and Educational Surveillance

There's a particular moment in my workshops on AI in education when I ask participants a simple question: "What information about your students do you currently collect, how do you protect it, and who has access to it?" The room typically falls silent for a short while before they speak up as educators realise they usually have clear, confident answers about their existing data practices. Then I follow with: "Now, if you implement an AI system in your classroom or educational institution, can you answer those same questions with equal confidence?"

The silence that follows is telling.

The Data Hunger of AI Systems

During my years in the technology industry, I learned something that every educator considering AI implementation should understand: Data is the lifeblood of these systems, and their appetite for information is pure unsatisfyingly greed. AI systems don't simply process the assignments students submit or track their test scores. They monitor keystroke patterns, measure time spent on tasks, analyse facial expressions through webcams, track eye movements, record voice patterns, and map behavioural tendencies across every digital interaction.

Consider what this means in practical terms. A student working on an essay isn't simply submitting written work for evaluation - they're providing the system with data about their writing process, their revision patterns, their moments of hesitation, their emotional state as captured through facial recognition, their engagement levels as measured by attention tracking. The AI system is learning not just about academic performance but about the student as a human being in ways that are both intimate and largely invisible to the student themselves.

This represents a fundamental shift from traditional educational data collection. When I assess a student's work, I see the final product and perhaps some drafts. I might notice if they seem stressed or excited during class. But I am not systematically recording, analysing, and storing data about their every micro-behaviour. The human relationship involves discretion, interpretation, and selective attention. AI surveillance involves comprehensive, permanent recording.

The Black Box Problem

One of the most troubling aspects of educational AI systems is their opacity. When I grade a student's paper or dissertation and they ask why they received a particular mark, I can explain my reasoning. We can discuss the criteria, examine specific examples, and even debate the assessment. This transparency is fundamental to educational integrity - students have a right to understand how they're being evaluated.

AI systems, particularly the "black box" solutions being marketed to educational institutions, offer no such transparency. They may provide a grade or recommendation, but the reasoning behind it remains hidden within proprietary algorithms. Even if vendors claim to offer explanations, these typically amount to statistical correlations rather than meaningful pedagogical reasoning.

I have witnessed this opacity firsthand when observing demonstrations of AI assessment tools. Sales representatives speak confidently about "sophisticated algorithms" and "machine learning optimisation," but when pressed for specifics about how decisions are made, they retreat to vague technical language or claims of proprietary protection.

Would you accept this level of opacity in any other aspect of your educational practice?

The Surveillance Creep

What begins as seemingly innocuous data collection inevitably expands. I have observed this pattern repeatedly in technology implementations across various sectors. Initial deployments focus on basic functionality - perhaps tracking assignment completion or identifying students who might need additional support. But once the infrastructure is in place, the temptation to collect more data, to monitor more behaviours, to predict more outcomes becomes irresistible.

Consider the trajectory we've witnessed in China, where educational AI systems have evolved from simple learning platforms to comprehensive surveillance networks. Students are monitored through facial recognition technology that claims to detect engagement, attention, and even emotional states. The rationale is always the same: We are doing this to help the students, to provide better support, to identify problems before they become serious. Yeah, sure!

But what happens when the definition of "problems" expands? When does monitoring for academic support become monitoring for compliance? When does data about learning difficulties become data about social attitudes, family situations, or political inclinations? The infrastructure doesn't change - only the uses to which it is put.

Imagine how excited Donald Trump would be to have a change to surveil students the same way the Chinese do and punish those who don't comply with his narrow-minded, authoritarian world-view.

The Myth of Anonymisation

One common response to privacy concerns is the assurance that data will be "anonymised" or "aggregated" to protect individual privacy. This response demonstrates either ignorance or deliberate deception about the realities of modern data analysis.

Contemporary AI systems excel at identifying individuals from supposedly anonymous data. Combinations of behavioural patterns, performance characteristics, timing data, and usage patterns create unique fingerprints that can be linked back to specific individuals with remarkable accuracy. The notion that removing names provides meaningful privacy protection is fundamentally obsolete.

Moreover, the most valuable educational data for AI systems is precisely the kind that must remain linked to individuals to be useful. Personalised learning requires personal data. Adaptive assessment requires tracking individual progress over time. The core functions that make educational AI appealing are incompatible with genuine anonymisation.

Cultural and Legal Variations

One of the most striking aspects of my research into global AI implementation has been the dramatic variation in privacy protections and cultural attitudes toward surveillance. In Estonia, strong digital infrastructure has enabled widespread AI adoption, but within a framework of relatively robust privacy protections. In France, the AI4T project demonstrates how educational AI can be implemented with transparency, accountability, and genuine respect for privacy rights.

Contrast this with implementations in China, where comprehensive surveillance is not a side effect but a primary purpose. Students understand that their every action is monitored, recorded, and analysed not just for educational purposes but for social control. The same technologies that promise personalised learning in democratic contexts become tools of authoritarian oversight in others.

In the United States, the situation is more complex but perhaps more concerning. Weak federal regulation means that private companies often have free rein to collect and use student data with minimal oversight. The protection of commercial interests frequently takes precedence over privacy rights, leaving students and families with little recourse when problems arise.

With the initiatives the current trump administration is taking to get access to all sorts of data with the purpose to profile the population to identify people or groups who are in opposition to emperor trump. From the US we have learned that data privacy doesn't exist if the legal framework is weak, which is the case in the USA today.

The Consent Fiction

Educational institutions often claim that privacy concerns are addressed through consent mechanisms - privacy policies, terms of service, opt-in checkboxes. This approach represents a fundamental misunderstanding of the power dynamics involved in educational settings.

Students, particularly younger learners, cannot meaningfully consent to comprehensive data collection when they don't understand the implications, when opting out means being unable to participate in required educational activities, or when the consequences of data sharing may not become apparent for years. Even adult learners face pressure to accept terms they haven't fully read or understood in order to access educational opportunities.

Furthermore, the complexity of modern data sharing arrangements means that even well-intentioned privacy policies often fail to capture the reality of how student data is actually used, shared, and potentially sold. When I examine the privacy policies of educational technology companies, I consistently find language that is either impossibly vague or incredibly broad, granting permissions that most educators and students would find shocking if they understood the implications.

The Emotional Dimension

Beyond the technical and legal aspects of privacy lies an emotional reality that's often overlooked in discussions of educational AI. Students need to feel safe to take intellectual risks, to ask questions that might seem foolish, to struggle with concepts, to express unpopular opinions. This psychological safety is fundamental to effective learning.

Comprehensive surveillance, even when justified by educational benefits, changes the emotional landscape of learning. When students know that their every hesitation is recorded, their every mistake catalogued, their every interaction monitored, they may become more cautious, more performative, more focused on appearing successful than on actual learning.

I have noticed this shift in my own students who have been educated in increasingly monitored environments. They are often more risk-averse, more concerned with giving "correct" answers than with exploring ideas, more focused on optimisation than on genuine intellectual engagement. This isn't necessarily the result of AI systems specifically, but it reflects the broader cultural shift toward surveillance and measurement that these systems both embody and accelerate.

A Framework for Responsible Data Governance

Given these concerns, how should educational institutions approach data governance in an AI-enabled environment?

I believe several principles should guide this consideration:

1. Minimal Data Collection: Collect only the data that's directly necessary for specific educational purposes. Resist the temptation to gather information simply because it is available or might be useful someday.

2. Transparent Processing: Ensure that students, parents, and educators understand exactly what data is being collected, how it is being used, and who has access to it. This transparency should be ongoing, not buried in lengthy legal documents.
3. Purpose Limitation: Use data only for the specific educational purposes for which it was collected. Resist pressure to expand usage or share data with third parties for secondary purposes.
4. Student Agency: Provide meaningful opportunities for students to understand, access, and control their data. This includes the ability to correct errors, understand algorithmic decisions, and opt out without penalty.
5. Vendor Accountability: Demand that technology providers demonstrate genuine commitment to privacy protection, not just legal compliance. This includes transparency about their own data practices, business models, and sharing arrangements.
6. Regular Audit: Continuously assess whether AI systems are providing sufficient educational value to justify their privacy costs. Be prepared to discontinue systems that don't meet this standard.

The Institutional Response

Implementing these principles requires institutional courage and commitment that goes beyond technical solutions. Educational leaders must be willing to ask difficult questions to tech vendors, to demand transparency that companies may be reluctant to provide, and to prioritise student welfare over technological convenience.

This means keeping vendor representatives out of decision-making processes, as I have emphasised throughout this book.

Their interests simply aren't aligned with student welfare, and their sophisticated sales techniques can easily overwhelm institutional decision-making processes. I usually recommend hiring an external project manager who is the gatekeeper and makes sure that the tech companies are kept away from the decision forums and that no vital information is shared with the tech companies. I will be happy to assist you in this phase so that you don’t get run over by the effective sales machines these tech companies have.

These companies work pretty much like restaurants in touristic areas. They have people on the street hijacking tourists and lure them into the restaurant. Once inside the restaurant they can wait a long time for just getting the menu. Tech companies are often no different. The prices are just a lot higher.

I was terrified to learn how Estonia has invited the tech companies all the way into the bedroom - the heart of the political decision process. Later I will look at how the students in Estonia have been influenced by massive use of technology in education. It is frightening reading.

It also means developing internal expertise about AI systems, privacy implications, and data governance. Educational institutions can't outsource these responsibilities to technology companies and expect their students' interests to be protected.

As we move forward in an increasingly AI-enabled educational environment, the choices we make about data governance and privacy will fundamentally shape the kinds of learning relationships we can maintain with our students. The question isn't whether we can implement AI systems while protecting privacy - it is whether we have the wisdom and courage to insist that we must.

14: The Individualisation Trap - Why AI's Vision of Learning Threatens Human Connection

The moment that crystallised my deepest concerns about AI in education occurred during a vendor demonstration I attended last year. The presenter, with obvious enthusiasm, showed us an AI system that could create completely personalised learning paths for each student. "Imagine," he said, his eyes gleaming with technological excitement, "a world where every learner follows their own optimised journey, at their own pace, with content perfectly tailored to their individual needs, available 24/7 from anywhere."

As I listened, I felt a growing sense of unease. This vision wasn't describing enhanced education - it was describing the systematic dismantling of everything that makes learning fundamentally human.

The COVID Lesson We've Already Forgotten

Before AI evangelists had captured the educational zeitgeist, we conducted a massive, involuntary experiment in individualised, technology-mediated learning. The COVID pandemic forced educational institutions worldwide into precisely the model that AI proponents now champion: flexible, personalised, available anywhere, adapted to individual schedules and circumstances.

The results were devastating. We didn't see liberated learners thriving in their optimised environments. Instead, we witnessed epidemic levels of depression, anxiety, and isolation amongst students of all ages. Academic achievement gaps widened along socioeconomic lines. Most tellingly, student wellbeing improved dramatically when institutions returned to in-person learning.

Yet somehow, this clear evidence that human connection is fundamental to effective learning has been forgotten in our rush to embrace AI-driven individualisation. The very model that proved psychologically damaging during the pandemic is being repackaged as educational innovation.

As mentioned earlier I find it particularly telling that Zoom, the company that arguably benefited most from the shift to remote interaction, mandated that their own employees return to physical offices because they recognised that creativity and innovation had suffered during remote work.

The Myth of Personalised Optimisation

The language used to describe AI-driven personalisation reveals a profoundly mechanistic view of learning. Students become "learners" to be "optimised." Education becomes a process of "content delivery" along "customised pathways." Learning becomes the consumption of "personalised resources" measured by "adaptive assessments."

This terminology isn't accidental - it reflects how AI systems conceptualise education. From an AI perspective, learning is essentially a data processing problem: input information, track performance metrics, adjust parameters, optimise outcomes. The model assumes that if we can collect enough data about individual learners and apply sufficient algorithmic sophistication, we can engineer optimal learning experiences. But we human beings are not like that. And our preferences and means of motivation and demotivation changes all the time depending on intrinsic feelings and external factors. All these factors don't fit into any algorithmic model at all. The beauty og being human – right?

But this mechanistic view fundamentally misunderstands how we humans actually learn. Learning isn't simply information absorption that can be optimised through algorithmic customisation. It is a social, emotional, and cultural process that emerges from interaction, challenge, surprise, and human connection.

Consider how you have learned the most important things in your life. Was it through perfectly optimised, personalised content delivery? Or was it through conversations with mentors, collaboration with peers, exposure to challenging ideas that initially seemed uncomfortable, moments of confusion that led to breakthrough insights? The most transformative learning experiences are often the least predictable - precisely the opposite of what algorithmic optimisation provides.

One of my favourite sayings – by Nelson Mandela - goes something like this:

You either succeed or you learn.

We learn the most when we are pushed outside our comfort zone and have to deal with a certain level of uncertainty and risk.

The Social Construction of Knowledge

One of the most profound insights from decades of educational research is that knowledge isn't simply transmitted from teacher to student or absorbed from content resources. It is socially constructed through interaction, dialogue, debate, and collaborative exploration. We learn not just from information but from seeing how others think, grapple with ideas, make connections, and overcome difficulties.

In my business school classes, which predominantly serve experienced professionals, I have observed this social construction of knowledge repeatedly. The most powerful learning moments occur when participants share their experiences, challenge each other's assumptions, build on partial insights, and collectively develop understanding that none could have achieved individually, and when they gain the courage to make decisions based on incomplete information, but where they have trust in relationships.

These professionals don't need me to deliver personalised content based on their individual learning profiles. They need facilitation of discussions that help them make connections between their experiences and new concepts. They need exposure to perspectives different from their own. They need the creative friction that comes from intellectual disagreement and collaborative problem-solving.

An AI system, no matter how sophisticated, cannot replicate this dynamic social process. It can provide information, track progress, and adapt content, but it cannot create the rich interpersonal and highly emotional learning environment where knowledge is collectively constructed and individually transformed.

The Collaboration Deficit

Perhaps the most troubling aspect of AI-driven educational vision is what it systematically excludes genuine collaboration.

Every AI-in-education scenario I have encountered focuses relentlessly on individual learners and their personalised experiences. The language is consistently about "self-paced," "self-directed," "individualised," and "customised."

This represents a profound impoverishment of educational possibility. Learning to work effectively with others - to negotiate differences, build on diverse strengths across different cultures and emotional realities, manage conflicts, create collective solutions - is arguably more important in our interconnected world than any specific content knowledge. These collaboration skills cannot be developed through individualised interaction with AI systems, but only by taking risks with other people – have confidence in other people.

I have noticed a troubling trend amongst students who have been educated in increasingly individualised, technology-mediated environments. They often struggle with group work, seem uncomfortable with intellectual disagreement, and approach learning as individual consumption rather than collective creation. They have been optimised for individual performance but underprepared for collaborative reality.

The Emotional Intelligence Gap

Supporters of and advocates for AI personalisation often claim that these systems can become emotionally responsive, adapting to learners' emotional states through sentiment analysis, facial recognition, or voice pattern detection. This represents a fundamental misunderstanding of emotional intelligence and its role in learning.

Emotional intelligence isn't about detecting and responding to emotions - it is about understanding the complex interplay between emotion, cognition, and social dynamics. It involves empathy, cultural awareness, interpersonal sensitivity, and the ability to navigate complex, unpredictable human relationships. These capabilities emerge from lived experience and human connection, not algorithmic analysis!

Moreover, the kind of emotional "intelligence" that AI systems offer is essentially manipulative. They detect emotional states in order to influence behaviour, to keep learners engaged, to optimise performance outcomes. This isn't emotional support - it is emotional exploitation.

True emotional support in educational contexts comes from human relationships built on trust, understanding, and genuine care. It involves recognising not just what students are feeling but understanding why they're feeling it, what it means in their broader life context, and how to respond in ways that honour their dignity and autonomy.

Cultural Context and Local Knowledge

AI systems trained on vast datasets might seem to offer access to global knowledge, but they systematically miss the local, contextual, and culturally specific understanding that gives learning meaning and relevance. Education isn't just about acquiring abstract knowledge - it is about understanding how knowledge applies in specific cultural, social, and professional contexts.

I have experienced this limitation directly when working with international students from diverse cultural backgrounds. The insights that matter most often come from understanding how different cultural perspectives illuminate universal concepts differently. These nuanced, culturally situated insights cannot be algorithmically generated - they emerge from human interaction across cultural boundaries.

A typical cultural dilemma to exemplify this is about the importance of time. If you can't deliver 100% on time what is most important? Deliver 80% on lime or deliver 100% to late? Your answer is highly dependent on cultural and emotional factors and gives space for a lot of debate and the opportunity to realise that there is more than one truth. Learning to respect that diversity is a basic human skill that has to be developed through education.

We currently live in a world where the stupid people seem to have all the answers and all the intelligence people have all the answers.

That ia not something new. As Socrates said: "Wise is the man who knows he know nothing"

Furthermore, AI systems inevitably embed the cultural biases of their training data and development teams. When these systems are deployed in educational contexts different from those in which they were developed, they may systematically misunderstand or misrepresent local knowledge, values, and ways of knowing.

The Engagement Illusion

AI proponents often point to increased "engagement" metrics as evidence of their systems' effectiveness. Students spend more time on task, complete more activities, demonstrate more consistent participation. But this engagement is often artificial, driven by gamification mechanics and algorithmic manipulation rather than genuine intellectual curiosity.

When we, in Gugin, want to fuel our customers' creativity we often take them out for a walk in the mountains around where we have our offices in the French Alps. Hiking together in great nature stimulates creativity and curiosity in ways no IT system can facilitate.

True educational engagement involves intrinsic motivation, intellectual risk-taking, creative exploration, and the willingness to struggle with difficult concepts. It is often messy, inconsistent, and difficult to measure. It can't be optimised through algorithmic adjustment because it depends on factors that exist outside the learning system - personal interests, life experiences, the current physical environment, social connections, and individual meaning-making processes.

The kind of engagement that AI systems optimise for may actually undermine deeper learning by training students to respond to external stimuli rather than developing internal motivation and self-directed inquiry skills.

Towards Human-Centred Integration

None of this suggests that technology has no role in supporting learning. But it does suggest that we need to maintain clear priorities: technology should serve human learning relationships, not replace them.

This means considering AI tools that enhance rather than supplant human interaction - systems that help teachers better understand student needs, platforms that facilitate rather than replace collaborative work, tools that augment human judgment rather than substitute algorithmic decision-making.

It means insisting that personalisation serve social learning goals rather than replacing them. Perhaps AI can help identify when students with different perspectives should be brought together for discussion, or suggest resources that support collaborative projects, or help teachers recognise when individual students might benefit from peer mentoring.

Most importantly, it means rejecting the false choice between technological innovation and human connection. The future of education doesn't require choosing between personalised learning and social learning - it requires finding ways to support both within fundamentally human-centred educational relationships.

As we consider the role of AI in education, we must ask not just whether these tools can work, but whether the kind of learning they enable is the kind of learning we want to promote. Do we want graduates who are optimised for individual performance but unprepared for collaborative citizenship? Do we want learning environments that are efficient but emotionally impoverished? Do we want educational relationships mediated by algorithms rather than built on human understanding?

The answers to these questions will determine not just the future of education, but the kind of society we are preparing our students to create and inhabit.

15: Reclaiming Agency - A Practical Framework for Responsible AI Integration

After three decades spanning technology development and education, I have learned that the most important question isn't whether to adopt new technologies, but how to maintain human agency when powerful interests are working systematically to diminish it. The false AI revolution in education isn't primarily about technology - it is about control, autonomy, and who gets to make decisions about learning relationships. There are really important issues at stake here, which is why the tech companies have to be completely excluded from the decision processes in the education industry.

The Power Dynamics We Must Acknowledge

Before discussing practical strategies for responsible AI integration, we must acknowledge the profound power asymmetries at play. On one side, we have massive technology companies with virtually unlimited resources, sophisticated marketing capabilities, and business models that depend on capturing and monetising user data. On the other side, we have individual educators, students, and educational institutions with limited technical expertise and constrained budgets.

This isn't a fair contest, and pretending otherwise is naive. The technology industry's approach to education follows the same pattern we've seen in other sectors: create dependency, capture data, centralise control, then monetise the relationship. The language of "partnership" and "collaboration" obscures what is fundamentally an extractive business model.

During my years in the technology industry, I was part of teams that were remarkably sophisticated at influencing clients to buy products they didn't need, to solve problems they didn't have, using solutions that often made their situations worse rather than better. The techniques haven't changed - only the stakes have gotten higher when the clients are educational institutions responsible for student welfare.

The SFA Framework: A Decision-Making Tool

Throughout this book, I have emphasised the importance of rigorous evaluation before implementing any AI system. When working with clients I/we recommend using the so-called SFA framework - assessing whether proposed AI implementations are Suitable, Feasible, and Acceptable in your specific context.

Suitability asks whether AI actually addresses genuine educational challenges in your environment. Too often, institutions implement AI solutions to problems that don't exist or that could be better addressed through non-technological means. Before considering any AI system, clearly articulate the specific educational problems you're trying to solve and why other approaches aren't working.

Feasibility examines whether you have the technical infrastructure, expertise, and resources to implement and maintain AI systems responsibly. This includes not just the initial implementation costs but the ongoing requirements for data governance, system maintenance, staff training, and strict vendor management.

Acceptability considers whether the implementation aligns with your educational values and is acceptable to your key stakeholders - students, parents, educators, and the broader community. This assessment should include careful consideration of privacy implications, potential biases, and long-term consequences. That is why you have to start out by forming policies that are approved and understood by ALL stakeholders. You can say your policies are your AI constitution.

Each factor should be evaluated independently and honestly and it is often a good idea to have an external facilitator to keep the process on track and to make sure you cover all the aspects – also the more unpleasant ones. A system might be technically feasible and address suitable problems but still be unacceptable from a values or cultural perspective. Conversely, a pedagogically desirable system might simply not be feasible given current resources and constraints.

You will realise you will have to deal with a lot of dilemmas in the policy development process.

Maintaining Educator Autonomy

Perhaps the most critical aspect of responsible AI integration is ensuring that educators remain in control of educational relationships at all times. This means rejecting any implementation that positions AI as the primary decision-maker about student learning, assessment, or educational pathways.

In my international consulting work, I have observed successful AI integration in educational contexts where the technology remains clearly subordinate to human judgment. In France's AI4T project, for example, AI tools support teacher decision-making rather than replacing it. Teachers receive additional data and analytical insights, but they retain full responsibility for interpreting this information, making educational decisions, and maintaining primary relationships with students.

This requires what I call "defensive adoption" - implementing AI systems in ways that preserve rather than diminish human agency. This might mean choosing tools that provide information rather than making recommendations, systems that support rather than automate assessment processes, or platforms that facilitate rather than replace human interaction.

The Vendor Separation Principle

Another important lesson from my technology industry experience is that vendor representatives should never be involved in institutional decision-making processes about AI adoption. Their interests are fundamentally incompatible with student welfare, and their sales techniques are sophisticated enough to overwhelm institutional judgment.

This separation should be absolute during the assessment and decision-making phases. Institutions should develop their own criteria, evaluate their own needs, and make preliminary decisions about AI integration before engaging with potential vendors. Only after internal decision-making is complete should vendors be invited to demonstrate how their products might meet already-established requirements.

I have seen too many institutions begin with vendor presentations that shape their understanding of both problems and solutions. This approach virtually guarantees implementations that serve vendor interests rather than educational goals.

Data Governance as Educational Governance

Responsible AI integration requires treating data governance as a core educational responsibility rather than a technical afterthought. This means developing clear policies about what student data will be collected, how it will be used, who will have access to it, and how long it will be retained.

These policies should be developed by educators and educational leaders, not by technology staff and definitely not vendor representatives. The questions are fundamentally educational: What information do we need to support effective learning? How can we protect student privacy while providing appropriate support? What are the educational costs and benefits of different data practices?

I recommend adopting what I call "privacy by design" principles: collect only data that directly supports specific educational purposes, provide transparent information about data practices, give students meaningful control over their information, and regularly assess whether data collection practices are providing sufficient educational value to justify their costs.

And never share any information with vendors, not matter how friendly they may appear. They are only looking for your weak spots. They are NOT your friends.

Building Internal Expertise

Educational institutions cannot outsource responsibility for understanding AI systems to technology vendors. This requires developing of internal expertise about how these systems work, what their limitations are, and how they might impact crucial educational relationships. AI technology is potentially too damaging to be let left with the technology companies.

This doesn't mean every educator needs to become an AI expert, but it does mean that institutions need staff who can evaluate vendor claims, assess technical capabilities, understand privacy implications, and translate between technical and educational perspectives. I will often be a good idea getting independent advisors on board who can assess the risks and potential advantages from a different perspective.

I always recommend that institutions begin by developing this expertise before considering any AI implementations at all.

Send staff to training programs, engage with academic research on AI in education, participate in professional networks focused on responsible technology integration. Only when you have internal capacity to evaluate AI systems critically should you begin considering specific implementations.

I also recommend that you NEVER accept the IT-vendors offer for training and consulting. It is just a part of their selling strategy and you will never get an unbiased platform for making the right decisions.

As I have mentioned earlier. Listen carefully to the resistance. People resist because they care. If they didn't care they would just walk away.

Student Agency and Digital Literacy

Responsible AI integration must include explicit attention to student agency and digital literacy. Students need to understand how these AI systems work, what data they collect, how algorithmic decisions are made, and what their rights and options are in AI-mediated environments.

This is particularly important given AI systems' tendency to influence behaviour through recommendation algorithms and engagement optimisation. Students should understand how these systems work to influence their choices and should develop critical thinking skills that help them maintain autonomy in AI-mediated environments.

You would expect students at higher educations to be alert and conscious about the risks using advanced technologies. But surprisingly that is not always the case. Many say that this is how it is now, and there is nothing they can do about it.

Nothing could be further from the truth and it is your responsibility as professor and teacher to make sure they gain confidence in themselves and the choices they make.

In the EU we have – fortunately – regulations that try to protect the individuals, but the technologies and their applications will always be ahead of the legislations. That is why critical thinking and healthy scepticism is so important at all times.

I hope with this book, that I have helped raise the awareness level.

I incorporate these discussions directly into my teaching, helping students understand not just how to use AI tools, but how these tools use them. This includes practical skills like recognising algorithmic bias, understanding privacy trade-offs, and maintaining critical distance from AI-generated recommendations.

Assessment and Continuous Evaluation

Responsible AI integration requires ongoing assessment of whether systems are providing sufficient educational value to justify their costs and risks. This assessment should include not just technical performance metrics but careful attention to impacts on educational relationships, student wellbeing, and institutional values.

I recommend establishing clear criteria for success before implementing any AI system and committing to discontinue systems that don't meet these criteria regardless of sunk costs or vendor pressure. This requires institutional courage, but it is essential for maintaining focus on educational rather than technological goals. As mentioned earlier you should always do a SFA analysis – the analysis where you analyse suitability, feasibility and acceptablility independent of each other. This way you have a much better chance of making an educated decision. All solutions you choose must be both suitable, feasible, and acceptable.

Regular evaluation should include input from all stakeholders - students, educators, parents, and community members. Their perspectives on whether AI systems are enhancing or undermining educational relationships should carry significant weight in continuation decisions.

And again – NEVER turn down resisters. Listen and understand. They usually have a good point.

Global Perspectives and Local Values

One of the most important insights from my research into international AI implementations is that there's no universal model for responsible integration. Different cultural contexts, legal frameworks, and educational values require different approaches to AI adoption.

Estonian approaches that work well in a small, technologically sophisticated, culturally homogeneous context might be inappropriate in more diverse settings. Chinese models that prioritise state control would be unacceptable in democratic contexts. American approaches that prioritise corporate freedom might be problematic where privacy protection is valued more highly.

This means that responsible AI integration requires careful attention to local values, legal requirements, and cultural expectations rather than simply adopting "best practices" developed elsewhere.

The Alternative Vision

Rather than rejecting AI entirely, I prefer to advocate for what might be called "tool-appropriate" integration - using AI systems where they genuinely enhance human capabilities without replacing human judgment or undermining human relationships.

This might include AI tools that help teachers identify patterns in student work that might otherwise go unnoticed, systems that facilitate rather than replace peer collaboration, or platforms that provide additional resources to support human-designed learning experiences.

The key distinction is maintaining clear hierarchy:

- Humans make educational decisions, AI systems provide information and support.
- Humans maintain primary relationships with students, AI systems provide supplementary resources.
- Humans assess student learning, AI systems provide additional data points for human consideration.

A Call to Action

I think the future of AI in education won't be determined by technological capabilities or vendor marketing campaigns – I think it will be determined by the choices that educators, students, parents, and educational leaders make over the next few years. These choices will establish precedents, norms, and expectations that will shape educational relationships for decades to come.

This is why the current moment is so critical. We are not simply deciding whether to adopt particular over-branded technologies; We are deciding what kind of educational relationships we want to maintain, what values should guide educational decision-making, and who should control the fundamental processes of teaching and learning – the educators or the technology companies?

The technology industry would prefer that these decisions would be made quietly, institution by institution, with minimal public discussion and maximum vendor influence. They benefit when adoption happens gradually, driven by competitive pressure and fear of falling behind, rather than through explicit democratic deliberation about educational values and priorities.

But we do have alternatives. We can insist on transparent public discussion about AI in education. We can demand that educational leaders explain their decision-making processes and justify their choices in terms of educational values rather than technological capabilities. We can support institutions that prioritise student welfare over technological innovation and hold accountable those that don't.

Building Resistance Networks

One of the most important developments I have observed in recent years is the emergence of networks of educators who are sharing information, resources, and strategies for maintaining human-centred education in an increasingly technological environment. These networks provide alternatives to vendor-dominated conferences and publications, creating spaces for honest discussion about both opportunities and risks.

I encourage every educator reading this to seek out or help create these networks in your local context. Share experiences with AI implementations, both positive and negative. Discuss practical strategies for maintaining educational autonomy. Support colleagues who are asking difficult questions about technological adoption.

These networks are essential for developing collective wisdom about responsible AI integration and for providing alternatives to the individual decision-making processes that vendors prefer to influence.

The Long View

When I reflect on my career journey from technology development to business consulting and higher education, I am struck by how often technological predictions prove wrong while human needs remain constant. The specific technologies that dominated industry attention during my early career have largely disappeared, but the human needs they claimed to address persist.

Students still need human connection, intellectual challenge, emotional support, and preparation for collaborative citizenship. Educators still need autonomy, professional judgment, and meaningful relationships with students. Educational institutions still need to balance innovation with stability, efficiency with effectiveness, individual needs with collective welfare.

These enduring needs should guide our approach to AI integration rather than being subordinated to technological possibilities. The question isn't what AI can do, but what AI should do in service of lasting educational values.

Some reflections to make

As I conclude this chapter, I want to return to a personal observation that has shaped my entire approach to AI in education. Throughout my career, I have had the privilege of learning from thousands of students across many countries and educational contexts. The moments that have been most transformative - for them and for me - have invariably been moments of profound human connection.

A breakthrough insight emerging from classroom discussion. A student sharing a personal experience that illuminates a complex concept for others. A moment of intellectual vulnerability that opens new possibilities for learning. The gradual development of trust that allows for genuine intellectual risk-taking.

These moments cannot be algorithmic. They cannot be optimised, automated, or scaled. They require human presence, emotional intelligence, cultural sensitivity, and the kind of intuitive understanding that emerges from years of educational experience.

AI systems may be able to supplement these relationships, to provide additional resources and support, to handle certain routine tasks. But they cannot replace the fundamentally human core of educational relationship without fundamentally changing what education means.

The Choice Before Us

We face a choice that will define education for generations to come. We can allow AI integration to proceed according to vendor timelines and commercial priorities, gradually ceding control over educational relationships to algorithmic systems. Or we can insist on maintaining human agency, using AI tools where they genuinely serve educational purposes while protecting the human elements that make learning transformative.

This choice won't be made once, definitively, but through thousands of smaller decisions made by educators, administrators, students, parents, and policymakers over the coming years. Each decision to prioritise human judgment over algorithmic efficiency, each choice to maintain transparency over technological sophistication, each commitment to student welfare over commercial interest contributes to preserving education's essentially human character.

The stakes couldn't be higher. We are not just deciding how to integrate new technologies into existing educational practices. We are deciding what kind of human relationships we want to preserve, what values should guide the preparation of future citizens, and whether education will remain a fundamentally humanising endeavour or become another arena for technological optimisation.

I believe we can choose wisely, but only if we approach these decisions with the critical thinking, collaborative deliberation, and commitment to human welfare that represent education at its best. The future of learning isn't predetermined by technological capabilities - it is up to us to create.

The choice is ours, but we must choose consciously, courageously, and soon.

References

Bibliography

MIT Brain chatGPT Study: Kosmyna, N., Maes, P., Ochoa, X., Han, C., & Caggianese, G., Your brain on ChatGPT: Accumulation of cognitive debt when using an AI assistant for essay writing task, 2025

Gallup-Meta Global Survey: María Florencia Melo, One in Four Young People in the World Feels Lonely, 2025

HolonIQ Research Team: , Five applications of artificial intelligence in education, 2019, https://www.holoniq.com/notes/five-types-of-artificial-intelligence-in-education

Isolation: Smith, A., & Jones, B., Remote instruction adversely impacts parental mental health, less among homeschoolers, 2023

longitudinal study: Madigan, S., Browne, D., Racine, N., Mori, C., & Tough, S., Association between screen time and children's performance on a developmental screening test., 2019

This paper reports: Kosmyna, N., Maes, P., Ochoa, X., Han, C., & Caggianese, G., Your brain on ChatGPT: Accumulation of cognitive debt when using an AI assistant for essay writing task, 2025

Apple's own 2025 research report: Li, E., Larsen, A. B. L., Zhang, C., Zhou, X., Qin, J., Yap, D. A., … Elman, J., Apple Intelligence Foundation Language Models: Tech Report , 2025

well documented: Chen, J., Dong, H., Wang, X., Feng, F., Wang, M., & He, X. , Bias and debias in recommender system: A survey and future directions (arXiv:2010.03240), 2020

Table of Figures

www.ingramcontent.com/pod-product-compliance
Ingram Content Group UK Ltd.
Pitfield, Milton Keynes, MK11 3LW, UK
UKHW022025041026
15591UKWH00012B/490